Becoming the

Millionaire
Employee

Becoming the

Millionaire Employee

HOW TO BECOME RICH WHILE WORKING FOR A PAYCHECK

ROGER SMITH

M

Modelbenders Press

For information address Modelbenders Press, P.O. Box 781692, Orlando, Florida 32878.

Modelbenders Press books may be purchased for business and promotional use or for special sales. For information please contact the publisher.

PRINTED IN THE UNITED STATES OF AMERICA

Millionaire Employee and its logo, the stylized ME are trademarks registered to Roger Smith. The Yabut term is a Service Mark registered to Roger Smith. Visit our web site at www.modelbenders.com

Designed by Adina Cucicov at Flamingo Designs

The Library of Congress has cataloged the paperback edition as follows:

Smith, Roger
    Becoming the Millionaire Employee /
    Roger Smith. – 2nd ed.
    1. Career – Management   2. Success – Lifestyle   3. Money – Behavior
    4. Millionaires – Behavior   5. Businesspeople – Conduct of Life   I. Title

ISBN-13: 978-0-9823040-1-3
ISBN-10: 0-9823040-1-3

Table of Contents

Introduction

Good morning future millionaires!

If you live in America, have a college degree, and have not been crushed by debt or a criminal record yet, then you are the prime slice of society who will make up the ranks of future millionaires.

Has anyone called you a millionaire before? No? Why not? You are the perfect specimen of the future millionaire, but no one has told you that yet. No one has hinted that you are on a track to become rich. Instead, everyone you have dealt with has told you that you are headed for a good job, a lot of work, the risk of the real world, and the pressures of supporting yourself and your family.

That sounds terrible! All work, no fun, no big dream. And no plan for the future.

But, that is not a surprise. You have primarily been surrounded by three kinds of people:

- Your Family,
- Your Friends, and
- Your Teachers.

Your Family is focused on making you a good person with a stable life. They just want to make sure you don't totally screw up. If you graduate from college and get a job, they have done their job. As long as you don't end up in jail, on drugs, or dropping out, that is generally all they care about.

Your Friends are in the same boat that you are in. They don't know what lies ahead any more than you do. They don't know much about how the world works either. So they are not telling you how you can become wealthy and successful—because they don't know either.

Your Teachers and Professors are great people, but they intentionally avoided going out into the business world, or what they call "the real world". Turning a job into a career and a paycheck into a million dollars is totally foreign to them. They can't tell you how to do it.

So who is going to point the way? Where are you going to learn the habits that make the average employee into a millionaire?

America is the greatest place in the world to become a millionaire. There are currently 9 million millionaires in the world. 3 million of them are in the United States. America has less than 5% of the world's population, but we have 33% of the world's millionaires. The idea of becoming a millionaire employee is more real in the U.S. that anyplace else in the world. You have already started down the path to personal wealth and becoming a millionaire employee, just by being born and raised in this country.

Most books and seminars will tell you that you have to start your own business to become rich. That is not true. There are more millionaires in America who got there as employees than from any other source. We are going to explain how they did that. We are going to show you how you can do it too. You are going to build your own plan to become your own Millionaire Employee. You are going to know how to do it, how long it will take, and what dangers lie ahead of you.

Financial independence—the right way to earn, spend, save, and invest money are not taught at home. Money is a big secret in most people's homes. It is not taught in college. College focuses on history, mathematics, physics, education, and psychology. Even the business schools do not teach you how to manage your own money. They teach you to manage a business, or at best to manage a business' money. They teach you to make a company rich. They do not teach you anything about becoming personally rich. I know—I earned an MBA and a Doctorate from a very good business school.

Because this information is not taught to everyone, most people make the same two big mistakes. First, they mismanage all of the money they have and end up over their heads in debt. Second, they fall for clearly fraudulent get-rich-quick schemes simply because they have not been taught any better. In this small book you are going to learn not to fall into either of these two traps. You are going to learn a better way. I am going to show you a clear plan that you can implement.

The World Financial Crisis

The whole world is in a financial crisis. But what does that mean to you? If you are just getting started, how relevant are the problems on Wall Street and down at the local bank? How important is it that you cannot get a loan to buy a home right now? Does it matter that other people have lost a bundle on their homes and may be evicted?

At your age and position in life, most of this does not matter at all. Simply because you have not had the money to invest in the stock market or the real estate boom, you have skirted the big problems that many older people are facing right now. You should watch, listen, and learn. This will happen again and you should understand this crisis so you are ready for the next one in 10 years.

There have always been financial crises. When they occur the politicians, businessmen, and talking heads always stand up and proclaim how terrible everything is. It happened in 2008, 2001, 1982, 1975, 1960, 1939, and many times before that. Generally these are spaced out far enough that people have forgotten the last one. In 2001 it was Internet and technology stocks that were way over priced. In 2008 it was residential real estate.

This crisis means two things to you:

1) It may make it hard, but not impossible, for you to find a good starting job.
2) This is a fantastic time to buy your first home.
   (Note: In the first edition I said this was a fantastic time to start and investment portfolio. That advice was 100% correct. The stock market is up 50% since then.)

Let's talk a little about the first one—Your Job Opportunities.

Companies and governments did not just stop functioning when the crisis set in. They still do all of the work they were doing before. They are just being more cautious about adding people. They still need talent. They are still doing 80 to 90% of the work they used to do. Some companies are growing and launching new ventures. I started a new seminar business in the heart of the crisis. To get this business up and running I had to hire web designers, graphic artists, and advertising people. I had to buy advertising placement, rent hotel meeting spaces, and create printed books. Every company has these same kinds of needs if they continue operating during hard times.

The companies you hope to work for might be slowing down their hiring, but they are not stopping. You may have to wait a little bit, but you are not doomed.

My Start

I graduated with my Bachelors degree during a financial crisis:

- Companies were not hiring. A few were interviewing on campus, but they were just collecting resumes.
- Gas prices were high and there were shortages with long lines to fill up the car.
- The economy was not growing.
- Foreign policy was a mess. People laughed at America because the Middle East was pushing us around and we were not pushing back.
- My classmates took a number of unusual jobs: a clerk at Montgomery Ward, a Tennis Coach, a Housewife, a Teacher, or nothing. Exactly one person got a professional job at Lockheed Martin because her Dad was a manager there.

I am writing this book for young people who are just getting started for two reasons:

First, I am a self-made millionaire and I did it as an employee inside of large and small companies. I did it while taking the career path that 95% of you will take. I did not have any special advantages. I just discovered that the means and the path to wealth were laying right there in front of me and everyone else. But most of my coworkers were not paying attention to them.

Second, the most important step in accomplishing this was starting with a college degree. I speak to college graduates because I know how to start where they are and become wealthy. I want you to know how to do this right now instead of floundering for several years. Or never figuring it out at all.

My father was a successful small business owner. He and my mother owned and ran a dry cleaning shop in a small town. They were the classic Mom-and-Pop shop. I saw how hard he worked and did not want to sacrifice that much time every day for 40 years. He worked a minimum of 60 hours per week—and he loved all of it. But I wanted to play more than that, so I remained an employee all my life.

I started with a Bachelors degree in Applied Mathematics from Colorado State University. But, I graduated during a financial crisis when there were no professional jobs to be had. That meant that I was the only college graduate selling auto parts for Montgomery Ward at the local shopping mall. Everyone else had a high school diploma or less and I was the college kid that they made fun of. I spent nine months selling tires, oil, and fan belts—and trying to figure out a better path.

That better path was graduate school. One of my old professors helped me apply to a number of colleges. I went into Texas Tech University and emerged two-and-half years later with a brand new Masters degree in Statistics. But the most important thing was that I emerged during a new economic era. Everything had changed. Ronald Reagan was president and he was spending enough money on defense to bury the Soviet Union. There were defense and government jobs everywhere. It was like stepping out of a time machine. The economy had changed 100% and I had 6 nice job offers to choose from.

I started working as a tiny cog in a company of 100,000 employees. I was working at General Dynamics in Fort Worth, Texas. It was a giant aircraft manufacturing facility with 30,000 employees in one place. I had a professional salary, a pension plan, a 401(K), and insurance. Life was completely different from when I was selling auto parts for six dollars an hour.

While I was working at this job day-to-day I was also managing my education, job performance, career goals, spending, saving, and investing to get ahead. I did not want to just sit in the middle with everyone else. I made many mistakes. But more frequently I made the right choices. You will hear about both the good and the bad in this book.

My education was normal—I did not have the advantage of a Harvard, Yale, or MIT degree. I wish I had and I respect everyone who has that advantage. But most of us start with a good education that looks just like thousands of others when you read it in a resume.

But one important key was that I never stopped learning. When I needed to know something new for my job, I got a new certification or a new degree in that field. I now hold 6 college degrees as a result of that behavior.

Rules Of The Game

Welcome to the game of working and making money. There are rules to this game.

Do you know the rules of Football, Basketball, or Tennis?

Do you play any of these professionally? No. But you know the rules of play. Most of you either play these sports casually—or you watch them for entertainment. But you know the rules. You know what it takes to win. You know what is allowed and what is prohibited. You know what strategies work and can see when players are totally screwing up on the field? At the end of the game you can talk with friends about how well the game was played. You can second guess the coaches and players.

How many of you know the rules of business and money? Have you watched people play this game? Have you seen which players are doing a great job and which are screwing up? How many winning players do you know by name? How many "games" have you watched? How many hours have you been absorbed watching the game or reading about the game of making money? What are the rules of playing a successful game of business? What are the rules of becoming wealthy?

Most people have only the vaguest idea. These games are not televised even though the winners take away billions of dollars.

You are about to become a professional player in this sports league. Most people do not know the rules. Most people are not ready to play professionally. Most people enter this sport in the minor league and stay there for their whole lives. They think they are playing professionally because they are being paid. But they still have amateur skills. They start out playing poorly, do not know the rules, receive no coaching, and play like an amateur for the rest of their life.

This book is one of your first steps to learning the rules, receiving the coaching, and stepping up to the professional level of play.

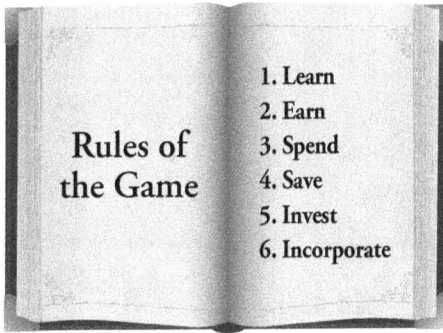

	Rules of the Game
Rules of	1. Learn
the Game	2. Earn
	3. Spend
	4. Save
	5. Invest
	6. Incorporate

Yabut

Throughout the book you are going to hear principles, rules, suggestions, and stories about becoming successful with your career and your money. Everyone has a different story. Everyone has a different set of circumstances. When I talk with successful people they all have their own stories—and they are usually very eager to tell those stories. All of them had reasons that they could have failed or given up. All of them worked with people who did give up, or who were afraid to start. All of them could have made their own excuses, but they chose not to.

All of them had a "Yabut". Some of them had a whole heard of yabuts surrounding them. The yabut is a hairy, ugly beast similar to a yak or water buffalo—but it is meaner and more sinister than any of them. It wanders around the wilderness of your life—generally peaceful and apathetic. But when something hard comes into your mind the yabut comes alive. It jumps up and attacks the thought of doing anything that is hard. It butts the idea until the idea is dead. It keeps attacking until the idea is dead or until you put a harness on it and hold it back.

You can always hear the yabut when it attacks. It makes the same sound right before it charges. It sounds like this,

> *"Yeah, but I can't afford to save a dime."*
> *"Yeah, but I don't have a job with a 401(K) plan."*
> *"Yeah, but you don't understand my situation."*
> *"Yeah, but ... "*

There are an infinite number of yabut attacks. They are all excuses for giving up. They all call for you to sit back down and do nothing. They are defending failure and attacking success. They will kill you and your future.

The Yabut can kill anything because it just keeps butting. Everyone has a Yabut in their heads. It attacks other people's ideas. It attacks your own ideas. It attacks any idea that threatens to put the Yabut to work. The Yabut wants you to sit down, lay back, take it easy, and be taken care of. The Yabut hates new, different, risky, or unknown ideas. It jumps and attacks all of these.

What will you do with your Yabut?

Will you let it run free? Or will you harness and control it?

I have not been able to kill my Yabut. But I have been able to control it so that it stops butting all of my good ideas. You will also have to get control of your Yabut if you want to get ahead in life.

What Is A Million Dollars?

If you want to become a Millionaire Employee, you might want to understand how big a million dollars is.

A million has always been the symbol of wealth and success. Inflation may have made it smaller. But it is still big enough to signify success. Those who reach it can always go further. They have broken the green glass ceiling and stand on the wealthy side of the world. They have the means to make more and to do it faster. If you make a million, you can probably turn it to $10 million.

But our goal in this book is to get you started toward that first million.

One million dollars is a 1 with 6 zeros after it. It is 1,000 times 1,000. So if you made $1,000 per year, you would earn a million in 1,000 years. Luckily you are going to earn a lot more than $1,000 in a year.

If you make $20,000 per year you will earn a million in 50 years.

At $40,000 per year you will get there in 25 years.

At $50,000 per year you will get there in 20 years.

At $100,000 per year you will get there in 10 years.

How far away is One Million?

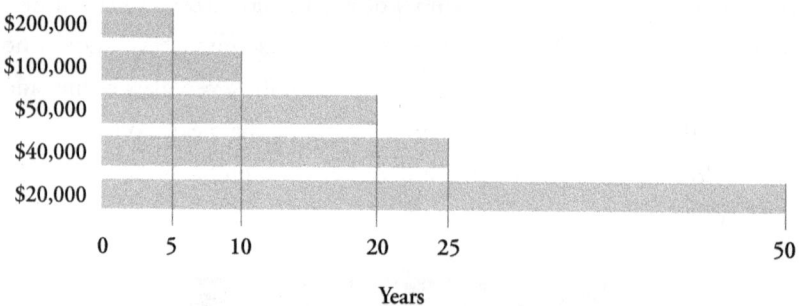

$200,000		
$100,000		
$50,000		
$40,000		
$20,000		

```
          0   5   10      20  25                      50
                         Years
```

Now that is something approachable. As college graduates you are going to start your professional life in the $30,000 to $50,000 range. Some of you will start even higher. Your average annual income over 20 years will be higher than $50,000. You will earn more than $1,000,000 in your career. Your college education almost guarantees that.

But our goal is not just to earn one million dollars. It is to save up one million or more so that you are a bonafide millionaire.

Compounding Your Income

In every home it is a challenge to get the children to keep their rooms clean. Parents order, threaten, bribe, and pay their children to do this. In one family the father told his two girls that he would pay them $1 each day if they made their bed, picked up their clothes, and put their toys away. But on a day that they did not do this they would not get paid. His daughter Amy eagerly agreed because she could think of a lot of things to spend that dollar on.

But his daughter Betty thought about it for a minute. And she made her dad a counter offer. She said she would like to be paid a penny for cleaning her room. And the second day she would like 2 pennies. The third day 4 pennies. And she would get double pay every day that she cleaned her room. But if she missed a day she would start over again at one penny.

Her dad thought this was curious, but he agreed. He thought Betty would learn a good lesson from this. He did not have much experience with math and did not know what he was getting himself into. The first day he paid Amy one dollar and gave Betty a penny. It did not feel fair to him. He felt bad for Betty. But he thought she would learn her lesson about money. Amy gloated and made fun of Betty. But Betty took her penny and put it in a piggy bank.

The second day Dad paid Amy another dollar and Betty got 2 pennies.

3rd day, Amy one dollar and Betty 4 pennies.
4th day $1 and 8 pennies.
5th day $1 and 16 pennies.
6th day $1 and 32 pennies.
7th day $1 and 64 pennies.

So at the end of the week Amy had earned $7. Betty had earned $1.27.

It was looking really bad for Betty and her dad offered to switch her pay to a dollar a day. But Betty said no, she wanted to stick with the doubling penny. During the second week Amy earned another seven dollars. Betty's pay started to pick up quite a bit. On Sunday she earned $1.28, which was more than Amy made for the first time.

On Monday Betty earned $2.56
Tuesday	$5.12
Wednesday	$10.24
Thursday	$20.48
Friday	$40.96
Saturday	$81.92

By this time Amy was furious that Betty was beating her so badly. Amy's total pay for two weeks was $14. Betty's total pay was $163.83. Betty's father was also getting worried that he had gotten himself into a bad deal. Luckily he was one of the early employees at Microsoft and he had enough money to keep his end of the bargain—at least for a little while longer.

By the end of the month Amy was earning a dollar a day and had accumulated $31. But on the 31st day Betty's daily pay was $10,737,418. Her total for the month was over twenty million dollars. Betty understood the value of compounding money. She knew how a small start can grow into a huge portfolio.

Betty Gets Rich with a Doubling Penny

Sunday	Monday	Tuesday	Wednesday	Thursday	Friday	Saturday
Today: 1¢ Total: 1¢	2¢ 3¢	4¢ 7¢	8¢ 15¢	16¢ 31¢	32¢ 63¢	64¢ $1.27
$1.28 $2.55	$2.56 $5.11	$5.12 $10.23	$10.24 $20.47	$20.48 $40.95	$40.96 $81.91	$81.92 $163.83
$163.84	$327.68	$655.36	$1,310.72	$2,621.44	$5,242.88	$10,485.76
$20,971.52	$41,943.04	$83,886.08	$167,772.16	$335,544.32	$671,088.64	$1,342,177
$2,684,354	$5,368,708	$10,737,418	**Total After 31 Days $21,474,836**			

This is a secret that most people do not understand. The small amounts that you can save today will add up to much more than you can imagine. Pennies in a jar at home are not the same as pennies in an investment that is growing. Compounding is the path to becoming a millionaire for most employees. You may earn over a million dollars in your life. But you are not going to be able to save all of it to become a bonafide millionaire. You are going to need the help of compounding to get there.

You need to think like Betty.

How Many Paths?

How many ways are there to getting a million dollars?

There are the rare paths. These paths are for a very few people who have an exceptional talent or exceptional luck. Famous people are usually in this list. Tim Tebow is an incredibly talented football player. His personal skill is in great demand and it will make him rich very quickly. Outstanding singers and actors can also earn a million dollars very quickly. These are the people in the news—because they are so exceptional, so unusual, so unique. These are not paths open to most people.

1) Professional Athlete
2) Hollywood Actor
3) Top Singer or Performer
4) Create a Cultural Trend
5) Inherit from a Rich Relative
6) Win the Lottery
7) Befriended By a Looney Millionaire
8) Become a Wall Street Banker
9) Invent Something Huge

The average person needs a different kind of path, a different kind of hope than these rare people have.

Mark Victor Hansen wrote *The One Minute Millionaire.* In that book he suggests that for the average person, there are only three paths to wealth.

1) Start, Own, and Run a Business,
2) Invest in Real Estate, and
3) Create an Internet Scheme.

All of these are open to average people. But he missed the biggest one of all:

4)   Become a Millionaire Employee.

There are more people who have become millionaires in the course of their employed life than through any other means. But they are considered so average and so mixed in with the general population that they are often ignored.

This is the path that I am teaching you to start on because it is the path that is accessible to the most people. Hansen's three paths are all correct but they are not accessible to everyone. My father started and ran his own business. I chose not to follow that path because I wanted a different lifestyle. But that does not mean that the door to millionaire status is closed to me. It means that I am taking the Fourth Door.

Rule 1:

Learn

Because you are a college graduate—or are about to become one—you have taken a powerful first step toward becoming a millionaire. It is one of the most important things you can do. A college degree is one of the most valuable things you will ever earn in life. It gives you the power to lift yourself up out of an hourly, low wage job that has no benefits and very little future growth.

Once you hold a college degree in your hands you are qualified for many salaried, good paying jobs that come with insurance and retirement plans. Beginning there is a huge step above trying to become wealthy without a college degree ... trying to become wealthy while strapped to a basic hourly wage. It is impossible to overstate how important this beginning is for you. If you do not have a college degree, but have the brains to do it, then I recommend that you stop reading right now. Get on a web site and find out how to get into a degree program at your local college. Contact the financial aid office and they will help you find all of the loans and grants that can make college affordable for you. Please stick to the state colleges with reasonable tuition and a good reputation. Most for profit colleges are not worth the high priced tuition they charge.

Education has been one of the secrets of success throughout Europe for centuries. Before that it was the Arabic and Chinese people who built their entire civilizations on education. But countries and cultures change. When they forget the importance of education and replace it with mysticism and dogma, they experience a sever decline in the quality of living and the power of their nation in the world. Other countries are figuring this out all the time. China and India jump-started their economic engines with low wage, low skill jobs. They make all of the junk you buy and they provide the basic customer services behind those products. When you call 1-800-HELPME you are usually talking to someone in India.

But once those countries were up and running—they needed to take the next step in building a modern, world-class, country. That step required **education**. It required high quality elementary schools, high schools, colleges, and graduate schools. It meant getting more college graduates into their population and fewer manual laborers. Today, China produces nearly 3 million college graduates every year. India produces over 1 million. They're onto one of the biggest secrets of America's success … **learning** … formally … informally … and throughout your whole life.

You are already part of this big secret. You are going to use your education to have a great career, a really fun life, and to become rich all at the same time. You are positioned to make that happen. You are reading this book to equip yourself with the professional and financial knowledge you need to get to that goal as soon as possible.

I teach these ideas to college students and college graduates for a good reason. It is because I understand the opportunities that lie ahead for you. I know the absolute importance of a college degree. I DO NOT recommend trying to get ahead without a college degree. The odds are just stacked against you if you do. But with a college degree, the odds are stacked in your favor. Society, history, culture, and psychology are all structured to give a college graduate special advantages, perks, and benefits that are not available to everyone else. You can choose to take advantage of that. Or you can try to fight against it.

Most of the people who teach personal and financial management and success methods are college educated. Most of them used the advantage of their college education to get ahead. I am the only one who goes directly into the college environments because I have a special affection for college students. I have spent more time in college than anyone I know. I added a new degree every time I found a professional challenge that required a new kind of knowledge or skill. It was a way of improving my performance at work immediately, while also preparing for a much bigger future.

School And More School

Like most of you I finished my Bachelors degree and was ready to head out into the work force. I just wanted to put classes, homework, and tests behind me. I wanted to earn really good money and spend my weekends having fun. But that is not what Mr. Economy had in mind for me. I graduated during an economic crisis. It was very similar to the recent recession. I could not find the kind of job I wanted. The companies that came to campus were not really hiring. The class of students I graduated with ended up taking hourly sales jobs at the mall, coaching tennis, teaching school, and returning to house work. The economy was putting all of our goals to get started with life on hold. It forced all of us to come up with alternative plans.

I graduated from Colorado State University with a Bachelors degree in Applied Mathematics. But it was impossible to find a job. At one point I went to Denver for a week and stayed with my roommate's parents. I lived in their basement and spent all day every day for a week driving to every single technology company in town asking for an interview and leaving resumes. I received absolutely no responses from this. I had graduated in the wrong place, at the wrong time, with the wrong degree. It looked like the American system of success had failed me. But that is not the end of the story.

I went back to my minimum wage job at Montgomery Ward selling auto parts, oil changes, and tires. But every day I was trying to figure out my next step. Where do I go from here? How do I "Make It"? One day it hit me … **graduate school**. I would go back to college for another degree. I called one of my professors, and asked her for advice and pointers to some good graduate schools in mathematics. This was "BI"—Before Internet. With her help I applied to several colleges and was accepted into Texas Tech University. I was going to become a Red Raider (their mascot) and learn more about mathematics—at least enough to get a job. I moved to Lubbock, Texas and began the life of a graduate student putting himself through school while working as a teaching assistant. They assigned me two freshman math classes to teach every semester and paid me more than I was making at Montgomery Ward. All of the other teaching assistants were complaining about how hard it was to live on the pittance they were paying us. I felt like I was making a million dollars. I had enough to pay my bills and to eat something besides peanut butter sandwiches or macaroni and cheese.

A bad economy can put a stumbling block in front of you. But it can't stop you from trying. You can find a way around it, over it, or through it if you just keep stumbling.

When I got out of graduate school with a new Masters degree in one hand and my old Bachelors degree in the other, I had lots of job offers. I felt like a rock star—everyone wanted to hire me. What a huge relief. And what a huge reward.

You can become wealthy without a degree. You can remain poor with a handful of degrees. But skipping college does not make it easier. It makes getting wealthy much harder. It limits the number of options you have. It generally exposes you to more risks from life. It can leave you in a position without insurance, without investment support, and without some level of earnings security. So pat yourself on the back because you have made one of the best decisions of your life by going to college and by sticking it out until you earn a degree.

Some of you just can't "do college". It might not be in your DNA, you might have family members you have to support, you might not have the grades, or you might have a job or business that is doing very well. If that is you—then that will just have to do. You can still use all of the advice in the book, but you may find the road a little tougher.

Education System

The Education system in the United State is an Industrial Age system. In spite of how wonderful it is, it is not the place to learn everything you need to know. They do not have a good balance of all of the knowledge that you need. They place an equal value on every course and every degree by charging the same tuition for all of them. There is an implication that all knowledge is equally valuable. That is not true. Each type of knowledge has a different kind and level of value. Some knowledge is valued in dollars. Other knowledge is valued in human contribution. And some is valued in its ability to stabilize society. You need to understand how the world values the knowledge you are pursuing. You do not want to spend four years and thousands of dollars acquiring knowledge that does not payoff in the kind of advantages that are important to you.

College is a system for conveying the most valuable knowledge of the world to all of the people who come through the doors—without knowing what they plan to do with that knowledge in their own lives. It is for giving you the tools that have been created over thousands of years. Without this you are starting from scratch trying to figure it all out on your own.

In a later chapter I will introduce you to Charlie Munger. One of his key principles for **failing** in business is for you to try to figure out everything on your own and to avoid learning from the billions of people who have gone before you.

If that is a principle for failure—then education is one of the key principles for success.

Knowledge In The Market System

The Market system is an Information Age system.

It pays for knowledge that helps the system survive.

It pays for knowledge that defends the system.

It pays for knowledge that keeps the system working every day.

It pays for knowledge that helps the system grow.

But most of all it pays for knowledge that helps the system **GROW**. Growth is valued more than any other factor.

Did you know that society has a system that decides how much you **should** make? This has created the divide between professional and menial jobs. In the shared consciousness of our society we believe that professional jobs **should** get high salaries, generous benefits, and special perks. We also believe that menial jobs **should not** receive these benefits. I did not create this system. I did not say that it is right. I am just being honest in explaining it to you.

There are millions of people out there who look at you and your qualifications, and they have an immediate judgment of what you **should** get for that. Getting an education is moving you into a new category where everyone believes that you should get more.

Your college education demonstrates that you have the will and the ability to do something that is hard. They show that you can do something that most people won't do or can't do. It is also a great piece evidence that you can do many more hard things in your life. It moves you to a different maturity level, to a higher level of looking at the world, to a bigger perspective on what is happening, to a broader view of what you can do in the world.

Your education is evidence to you, employers, and the world that have what it takes to face difficult challenges, to tackle all of the work that they throw at you, and to achieve a goal that is several years in the future.

Around 300BC Aristotle said that, *"The educated differ from the uneducated as much as the living from the dead."* That is a very strong, even harsh, statement. And it was a distinction that Aristotle made over 2300 years ago. Society has become much more information based since then. If it was true then, then it is even more true today.

5 Steps To Education

There are at least 5 major steps in your education. Each of these steps contributes to your ability to function in the 21st century. Each step allows you to do more, to contribute more, to earn more, and to build more wealth.

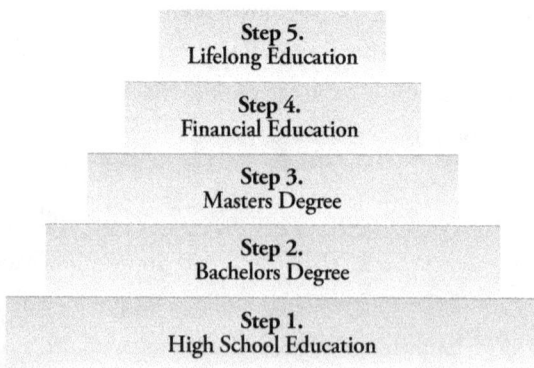

Step 5.
Lifelong Education

Step 4.
Financial Education

Step 3.
Masters Degree

Step 2.
Bachelors Degree

Step 1.
High School Education

Step 1. High School Education.

A high school education is the longest step because it takes you twelve years to achieve it. But it is the minimum you need to function in society. In the 19th century a High School education was all you needed to be one of the leading members of society. You were in the top 25% just by finishing high school.

My parents had just a little more than a high school education. Neither of them ever earned a college degree. They were the pillars of the community in the small town where I grew up. My father owned his own business. He was the local dry cleaner. He took some classes in accounting and was an avid supporter of the Dale Carnegie program for public speaking. But he ran his business, our family finances, and some parts of the city based on his High School education. Like most of his generation, the High School diploma was a ticket into business and to active leadership in the community.

Step 2. Bachelors Degree.

A bachelors degree is a much shorter step. It takes just four years to complete. But it is really the 20th century equivalent of the high school diploma of the 19th century. It puts you in the top 25%. For most people this is a necessary step for building wealth. It is one of the expected qualifications to be trusted with many responsible, high paying, benefits-carrying jobs. It puts you into a different level of earning, a different level of social protection, and a different level of understanding how society works.

In general, people with a college degree see a much broader and deeper world than those without one. This is not necessarily because college graduates are smarter. It is more because they have had the advantage of four more years of tutoring and mentoring by people who specialize in understanding the world and society. College professors are different from high school teachers in that they generally are trying to understand some part of the world in extreme detail. They are also the people who are explaining how the world works of formal journal publications. These people really do have a deep and mature view of the world which they can share with you in the four years that you spend in their hands.

Step 3. Masters Degree.

There has been a constant inflation of education. In the 21st century it has become much more common for people to earn a Masters degree. This jump takes two additional years. I earned my first Masters in the 20th century and used it to enter the defense industry. At that time it was very rare for the engineers and scientists to hold advanced degrees. Most people from the bottom to the top of the organization just had a Bachelors degree.

When I started my professional career as an Operations Analyst we were studying the performance of combat aircraft and a Masters degree was a rare asset. I was one of maybe ten people in a department of 150 who had a Masters degree and I can recall only two who had a Doctorate. Advanced degrees were very rare in the 1980's, but that has changed a great deal.

Today colleges are making graduate degrees much more accessible and millions of people are taking advantage of that. At a recent management society meeting I was talking to a bank teller who had a Masters degree. I was very impressed. It showed fantastic planning for the future on her part. She was working toward becoming a manager or officer of the bank while still sitting in the teller window. My neighbor ran his own career for 20 years before he put himself through both a Bachelors and a Masters program. Advanced degrees are popping up on resumes everywhere.

If you are just about to finish your Bachelors degree I would suggest that you make a note to begin a Masters program sometime in the next 5 to 7 years. You do not have to start right now. You might need a rest. I know I did. But don't give up on schooling at such a young age. You probably have some of your best learning ahead of you.

Given the economic situation that we are in right now, some of you will be faced with the choice of a minimum wage job or going back to school. Which do you think would be better in the long-run? Graduate school is an option that you need to consider.

Step 4. Financial Education.

Right now you have a lot of formal education and little money to manage. Most of you can learn more about money management than you can put to use, simply because you have no money. But eventually you will have a lot more money to manage. You will have saved and invested more money than you make in an entire year. When you reach that point, it will be important that you know how to handle that money so you don't lose it. You want to see it grow, not evaporate.

When changes in the economy can wipe out more than you make in a month or can earn you more than you make in a month, it will be important for you to know how to be on the positive side of these changes. Not on the negative side.

If you are going to save money you have to learn how to invest it. You need to learn about savings accounts, certificates of deposit, money market accounts, mutual funds, stocks, bonds, and real estate. As you accumulate enough money to take advantage of these you need to understand how they work and what the risks are.

You might choose to let someone else manage the details for you, but you need to understand what you are getting into. You need to know when each of these is right for you. There have been many millionaire musicians and athletes who knew nothing about investments. They entrusted it all to some manager and were wiped out either because the manager did stupid things with the money, or just plain stole it. You can't let that happen to you.

Step 5. Lifelong Education.

You are about to embark on a fantastic journey. Your career and your life are going to be filled with thrilling adventures and terrifying challenges. You are going to find some unusual opportunities. As your role in life changes, the kind of knowledge you will need is going to change. How are you going to deal with that change? How are you going to benefit from and prosper from that change?

Some people enter one company or organization and stay for their entire life. The company tells them what to learn for their next job. They might even be able to learn everything on the company's time. Staying inside of one organization can be safe that way.

But most of you will change jobs many times and you will even change career fields a couple of times. To do that successfully and to be in a position to take advantage of the opportunities that pop up, you have to be learning in new areas all the time.

I started my career with degrees in Mathematics and Statistics. My first job was in Operations Research with a company that made jet fighter planes—specifically the F-16 Fighting Falcon. We were all very proud of of this plane and what it could do for the nation. But over time my role changed. New opportunities popped up and I moved on. I found myself working as a computer programmer among people who had gotten their degrees in computer science. I learned a lot on the job, but I decided that I needed to learn a lot more if I was going to compete with them successfully. So I dug up opportunities to get a graduate degree in computer science. I was looking for a Masters program that I could do at night, on weekends, and while traveling. But I stumbled on a Ph.D. program and decided "what the heck", I might as well get a Ph.D. as another Masters degree. So I did that degree in 4 years while working and traveling. As a result, I was a computer scientist both in practice and by education. I changed my competency by adding to my education.

About eight years later I was working for a great company of 1,800 people. The founder and President of the company decided that he wanted to elevate some of the technical staff to the level of Vice President. In addition to the accountants, marketers, and retired military minds, he wanted more technical expertise in the circle of people who were guiding the company.

He also wanted to make a statement within the company. He wanted the engineers and programmers to know that they could become executives as well. So each Division Vice President nominated one or two people for these new positions. I was lucky enough, and prepared enough, and ambitious enough to be picked for one of the positions. The President, Ed Bersoff, selected seven of us to become Vice Presidents of Technology within the company.

I went to my first Executive meeting with butterflies in my stomach. Luckily I knew there were six more engineers in the room with the same butterflies. But after the first meeting it was clear that I did not know enough about business to be helpful at this new level. It was clear that I needed to learn more about accounting, contracting, organizational theory, and legal issues.

How was I going to do that? It looked like a good time for an MBA degree. So I was back in school years after I thought I had finished for my entire life. After two years working nights and weekends, I was holding formal degree number four.

You have a five step education plan ahead of you and behind you. You need a high school diploma. You need a bachelors degree. You may need a Masters degree. You certainly need a financial education. And you need to be learning all the time. You need to tackle new information, new ideas, and new knowledge whenever the challenges strike. Never sit down and say, *"I don't know how to do that and I am not going to learn to do it."* If it is on the path you want to follow, then you can, must, and will learn a new field.

Nothing is too hard for you. If you have gotten to where you are today, you can probably handle anything else that lies in your path to becoming a Millionaire Employee.

Salary And Education Are Aligned

Your salary and benefits generally align with your education.

When I was in college I worked at Montgomery Ward and Sears making minimum wage—about $5.50 / hour—or about $10,000 / year. I had no insurance, no 401(K) plan, and no one looking at me with a career plan in mind. If I had gotten seriously sick or injured I would have been ruined. The debt I could have been incurred would have followed me a lifetime.

In graduate school I was a Teaching Assistant for Freshman math classes. I earned about $1,000 / month for teaching 2 classes per semester. With the summer semester this was nearly $12,000 / year. I thought I was rich.

When I graduated with my Masters in Statistics I took a job at General Dynamics for $28,400 / year. Now I really was rich. Rich enough to enjoy all of the hobbies I was interested in. Rich enough to begin saving money to build wealth. I was also covered by insurance and had a 401(K) with 50% matching funds from the company.

Without a college degree it is very difficult, or even impossible, to get from $5.50 / hour with no benefits to $28,400 / year with benefits. That's a 300 to 400% jump.

Today those numbers are different, but the ratio is still the same or greater. A college degree will triple your earning potential. Adding a Masters degree can quadruple what you were earning as an hourly worker.

In my experience you cannot afford to try to become wealthy without a college degree. It is possible. If you read *The Millionaire Next Door* by Tom Stanley he will tell you the stories of all kinds of people who became wealthy. But in general, if you do **not** have a college degree, you have one path to wealth. You **have** to start your own company. You **cannot** do it as an employee if you do not become a professional, college educated employee.

Rule 2:

Earn

———◆———●———◆———

If you are a college student you are about to take on a professional job with a decent paycheck. If you are already in the professional workforce, then you are in such a job or are qualified to get such a job. This automatically places you in a better position than 90% of the people in the world. You are going to work in an environment that makes trillions of dollars every year, that is responsible for most of the progress in the civilized world, and that needs the help of energetic, smart, and motivated people like you to keep this machine moving.

The machine will reward you if you help it grow. But, if you do not help it grow, then the machine will grind you up like a dog chewing a bone. It will whittle you down over 10, 20, 30, or 40 years. In the end the machine will spit you out and leave you poor and alone in a nursing home.

Is that what you want? No.

Can you do better? Yes, certainly you can.

Are you already learning to do better? I hope so.

Would you like to be the next generation of movers and shakers who make the machine work better? Who make it grow?

Earning money as an employee is a direct result of what you do to make that machine **GROW**!

I didn't say it is a result of helping the machine to keep running. Reward does not come to the people who make sure the machine maintains its current speed. There are millions of dedicated employees who pour their hearts out to make sure that their organizations keep running day in and day out. These people **do not** get ahead. They are essential to keeping the business, government, and non-profit machines of the world working. But they are rewarded by the lowest amount of money and the fewest benefits that will keep them from quitting. No more than that.

The people who reap the big rewards are those who can make the company grow. They may learn this from someone who is already doing it in their organization. They may learn it from a book or seminar. They may learn it by watching the machine work. They may learn it by their own trial and error. But only those who learn to do this can reach into the machine and demand more compensation, more money, more perks, more support, more resources.

How do you do that? How do you make a company grow? You are just now getting started. What do you know that can really make a difference?

Showing Up

Let's start with Woody Allen.

Woody Allen is a skinny, nerdy, whiny kid from New York. He is a very unlikely success story. But during an interview, he was asked how he did it. And he said,

"Half the secret of success in life is just showing up!"

Now that is hilariously simple. It is also hilariously true. Half the secret to passing your college classes was just showing up for class. Half the secret of becoming a good golfer is just showing up to play. Half the secret to being successful at work is just showing up.

Here's a secret you might not have learned yet. It is a huge problem in most companies to just get people to show up for work every day. Companies are filled with people who have "special issues". They have an infinite list of reasons that they just can't get to work today. Or just won't be in until 9 or 10 or 11 o'clock. In a world where half of the people don't even show up to work to compete, you can be in the top 50% just by arriving.

Now you're thinking … that can't be true. If people did that, their bosses would just fire them. Oh, Really? Well some bosses have tried that. First, they found out how hard it is to fire someone in our society. And when they succeeded, they hired a replacement who didn't show up either. So after a few rounds of this they just gave up and figured out how to make the most of the people who did show up. They also figured out how to reward those who showed up. When the raises, bonuses, and perks roll in, there are 50% of the people who don't understand why they are not getting any of it. They really don't know. Because they were not around when the work was getting done! They were not around when the early birds were divvying up the worms. They never became part of the clique that was putting their dibs in for the cash.

So the first thing I am going to tell you about being successful at work is … just show up.

And also, show up early. Showing up late is just a little better than not showing up at all, and not nearly as good as showing up early.

There is no such thing as showing up "on time." There is only Early, Late, and a "Grunt".

What's a grunt, you might ask? There are two kinds of grunts. If you are a little bit past "on time" it is "humpf", which means *you stink*. If you are "on time" or a little bit early it is "hmmm", which means *who cares, you don't impress me*. You do not want to be either of these.

Half the secret of success in life is just showing up … and showing early.

Being Miserable

Charlie Munger is the partner of Warren Buffet at Berkshire Hathaway. Charlie and Warren are two of the richest people in the world. Warren is #1 and Charlie is only #387 with $2 billion. He gave a commencement speech at Harvard entitled *"Prescriptions for Guaranteed Misery in Life"*. He listed 4 guarantees for becoming miserable and for failing in business. Charlie's list was:

1) **Be Unreliable.** This will undermine and overturn all of the good built by every other trait. Do not show up for work, do not turn work in on time, do not communicate with other people, let deadlines slip, and generally do not meet anyonelse's expectations.

2) **Learn everything you possibly can from your own personal experience.** Totally minimize what you learn from the good and bad experiences of other people. Don't learn by reading or by talking to other people. Insist that you have to experience everything yourself. Insist that you have to make every mistake that everyone else has already learned from.

3) **Go down and stay down when you experience your 1st, 2nd, and 3rd big failures in life.** Don't get up again and keep trying because life is full of challenges that will surely keep you down. When you experience a failure, accept that you cannot handle life's challenges and settle for something less. Just stay down.

4) **Take everything you hear at face value.** Never step back and consider it objectively and unemotionally. Do not develop your own model of the world and your own principles to live by. Just let the world tell you what is true, what is best, and what you should do.

Charlie assures us that if we will just follow these four simple rules, then we can be comfortable in the misery of life. We can easily move from one miserable day to the next miserable day. We repel the joys we see in other people's lives and make sure those pass us by. Who knew it would be so easy? If misery can be defined in such a short list of rules, is it possible that happiness and success could also be defined by just four rules? Is it possible that the reverse of these very four rules will work to make us as happy as the rules make another miserable? Maybe personal and financial success are not that difficult after all.

Work All The Time You Work

Brian Tracy has an excellent saying. It is, *"work all the time that you work."* Yes, simply work when you are at work. This is second only to Showing Up in making you a leader and a top earner in your company and profession.

If just 50% of the people even Show Up dependably, then only a fraction of those that do show up actually do work. Most people show up at work fully prepared to take a break. The first thing they do is find the coffee and find some people that want to gossip. This chit-chat is about last night's television show, the big game, how the local teams are doing, who is having a sale, and of course, running down the local office scapegoat. What has so-and-so done wrong? How dumb are they? Can you believe what they wore to work? I heard that their son was arrested this weekend. Blah … blah … blah.

Then after the coffee, chit-chat, and gossip, they are ready to see what is happening in their email. Maybe something urgent came up and they should handle it right away.

Many of them are killing time until their first meeting of the day. In fact many people function only via meetings. They are not at all self directed. They genuinely do not know what to do that is beneficial to their company … unless they attend a meeting and are told what to do.

When they finish those assigned tasks, then it is back to the coffee and email until someone tells them what to do next.

This is a very passive and dependent approach to a job, a career, and earning top dollar. This is not going to work. Those people really are cogs in a machine. They cannot direct themselves, they have to be shown how to fit in, how to contribute.

Guess who is showing them? The people who **do** know how to get ahead. The people who do know what is good for the company. The people who are actively working without explicit directions. The people who **get it**. They **get it** in terms of the purpose of the organization. But they also **get it** in terms of the rewards that are handed out.

You can't get ahead by being the wandering worker. You need to be the working worker. Since you are new to the company a great idea is to go around and ask people what they do. Ask what the department does, or what their group does. Some of them can tell you the history of the company or the department or the local office. All of that knowledge will paint a more complete picture of what the company does—and it will give you some clues to what you can do to help.

Along the way you might also find some people to mentor you. They might ask you to help them. They might offer to give you advice and guidance. They might tell you about internal politics and the in-fighting that is happening.

You should accept the mentoring, guidance, and requests for help. But stay out of the politics and in-fighting. You are too new to be part of these fights. There's a saying in Africa, *"When the elephants are fighting, the other animals should stay out of the way."* You should stay out of the fights between the office elephants. If you try to mix it up, you are going to get trampled.

You may wonder why someone you just met would spend the time to give you advice, guidance, and some mentoring. It is because they are eager to help other people, but no one has given them the opening before. No one has ever asked them before. All of the young new employees think they know everything already. They think the older people are worn out and witless. They do not take the time to learn the history and the lessons that have accumulated in the company over 10, 20, 30, or 100 years. They assume that they brought with them everything they need to know to be outstanding in this job. That is a hallucination that they will eventually get over. But you can get over yours immediately and get started months or years sooner than everyone else.

What have you learned so far?

1) Show Up Reliably (ahead of 50% of the people)
2) Show Up Early (ahead of 60%)
3) Work all of the time you work (ahead of 70%)
4) Learn about the mission of the company from the inside (ahead of 80%)

That is a great start. With four simple rules of behavior you are already outshining and eventually outperforming 80% of the people in the office. And it wasn't that hard. Nor was it very complicated.

Your education is going to help you work all of the time you work. Recognizing all of the valuable work that can be done, will allow you to make the most of showing up regularly and showing up early.

These are all complimentary practices. Each one reinforces the others.

Effective

As you figure out the organization, you are going to find out that there are thousands of things that need to be done. Not all of them are equal. Your goal is to do the tasks that are the most valuable, you want to be effective with all of the work you are doing. You want your efforts to generate results that are valued.

It is easy to see all of the work that needs to be done and get busy doing work … work that is not important.

You might choose your work because it is easy, because it fits your personality, or because it fits your formal training. Before you start—try to figure out which tasks are really valuable. Which tasks will make the company grow? Then find ways that you can contribute to those.

In many cases, jobs that really do generate value are too hard for any one person to tackle alone. These are the tasks that you should be contributing to—and hopefully contributing in a visible way. How will you become part of the team that is working on these hard and valuable tasks? Maybe you have been talking to a lot of people about how the company works. Maybe you have picked up a mentor by showing interest in the company. Maybe one of the senior people will invite you onto the team. Or maybe that person would be open to you if you just asked them if you could join up. Maybe all of that advice on digging into the company, getting to know people, and asking questions really is going to pay off.

You are paid for results, not for effort. Getting into the important projects will move you to where the results are being created. It does not matter how hard or little you work—it matters how good your results are. Being off in some deserted and ignored project is not the place to be getting good results—that no one cares about.

Larry Winget suggests that you, *"Discover your uniqueness and learn to exploit it in the service of others, and you are guaranteed success, happiness, and prosperity."* (see his book, *Its Called Work for a Reason*) You bring unique talents to a job. You can contribute something that others cannot. You want to be giving that unique talent to a project that is valuable to other people, and especially to your boss and your company.

Tyranny Of The Urgent

Where ever you work—including school—you will find that there are URGENT tasks and there are IMPORTANT tasks.

Urgent tasks are the ones that call for your immediate attention. They fly into your cubicle and demand that you do something about them. You have a term paper due tomorrow and if you don't get at least an 80 on it, you will not pass the class. That is an URGENT task. You need to do it right now and the consequences are important. So this is both Urgent and Important.

Your boss throws you a list of names and tells you to call them all before the meeting on Friday. He wants them all to send in materials and be at the meeting. Your job is to make sure they all do it. That is urgent. It has an immediate deadline and you are responsible for making it happen. To the degree that you like this job and want to keep it, the task is also important because potentially you will not have this job if you do not do it.

When that same term paper or call list is due in 3 weeks, the task is still IMPORTANT, but it is just not Urgent any more. It really needs to be done and it would be good to do it now. But if you put it off, then nothing bad is going to happen ... at least not yet. It is Important but not Urgent, so you are working on it a little here and there. Maybe you set aside one Wednesday afternoon to spend 4 hours on it because you are very forward looking. You are taking care of what is Important and doing it early.

Tyranny of the Urgent

	URGENT	NOT URGENT
IMPORTANT	**1** Assignment Due Tomorrow	**2** Assignment Due Next Month
NOT IMPORTANT	**3** New Movie	**4** Clean Room

But then on Wednesday afternoon your friend comes flying into your room and says he has an emergency. His term paper is due tomorrow and he has not even started on it. He **has** to have your help or he will fail. Will you please come work with him and help him find references. This is an URGENT task. It has to be done now or the consequences will be terrible ... for him. This task is Urgent because it is flapping around your head and demanding attention. It is excited and loud and pleading. But it is NOT IMPORTANT ... to you. Your term paper is important to you, his paper is important to him. His term paper is Urgent to him, and he is trying to make it Urgent to you. What do you do?

That is a classic school example of what happens at work all the time. There are always lots of tasks to be done. Some are IMPORTANT to you and some are NOT. Some are URGENT to you and others are NOT. And there are those tough calls that are URGENT, but NOT IMPORTANT.

The final category is the tasks that are NOT URGENT and NOT IMPORTANT. Like watching the new episode of House or cleaning up your filing system. You can see all of this listed in the simple picture.

You can do all of these. But you need to guard against getting them in the wrong order. Your ability to be effective at work is going to be determined by your ability to consistently make progress in ONE of these categories—those tasks that are IMPORTANT, BUT NOT URGENT. These are the tasks that slip to the bottom of the stack. These are the tasks with the real long-term payoff that most people never get done. These are the tasks that can make a major difference in your earning power.

Most people are geared to address all tasks that are URGENT. Many people become experts at handling Urgent tasks. It does not matter whether they are important or not, they take on all of them. They are focused on items #1 and #3 in the figure.

But most people let the Important but Not Urgent tasks fall away. In doing this they reduce their effectiveness by 50% and do not work on their long-term goals. They are not prepared for the challenges and opportunities that come to them from higher up the organization or from an entirely different direction. By focusing only on Urgent tasks, they are just prepared to be the fireman who rushes to every fire. They are not ready to be the safety engineer who makes sure that there are no fires to begin with.

Put order in what you work on. Have control over where your time and energy is going. Address tasks in this order:

1) Urgent AND Important

2) Important BUT Not Urgent

3) Lend a helping hand to the Urgent BUT Not Important to Me (someone else's Important tasks)

4) Who cares about the others. If they are not Important to you and not Important to someone else, then who cares if they get done at all?

Valuable And Visible

Your contributions also need to be Valuable and Visible. If no one, especially your boss, can tell that you are doing something, then that almost completely negates the value of it. You are not trying to show off. But the work has to be noticeable. It has to be something that someone else cares about enough to say "good job" or "thanks a lot". There has to be something Important about it.

As you figure out which jobs are valuable and visible, you can ask to work on those. Just tell the project leader or your boss that you are interested in those jobs and would like to help with them. They may give you a shot right off. Or the job may already be fully staffed. But they will remember that you are eager to work on that project or that kind of job. Most people never say anything. They accept any assignment. They do what they are told. Then they wait at the coffee machine or in their email until they are told to do something else. The fact that you are showing an interest in the most valuable tasks and are asking to work on them will stand out.

Being eager and willing to work, showing up early and putting in a full day's effort will be noticed. It has to be noticed. So few people do it, that it cannot go unnoticed. Not noticing these traits would be like not noticing a tiger walking down your street. You just don't see it every day. It is rare. It is eye catching. It is important. People will notice.

When I left General Dynamics I moved to the suburbs of Washington DC to work for a small software company with only 100 employees. It was a huge change from 100,000 people to 100. The culture was totally different. The small company was full of people who were hungry to do impressive work. It was a personal hunger and everyone was striving to contribute something important.

When I received the offer letter it gave my salary as $55,000—which was a 40% increase over what I was making at General Dynamics. Wow, I was thrilled. I was flattered. But there was also a surprise in the letter. It said that I would be working a standard 45 hour week. That was a twist I had not heard before. But I was so pumped to go to this small company and to get the bigger paycheck that I accepted.

When I got there I learned that all of the programmers and managers were signed up for at least 45 hours/week. Some for even more. It allowed them to do more work in a week than their competitors and that productivity gave them the cash they needed to pay better salaries than the competitors.

I quickly learned that those five extra hours allowed me and others to do 40 or 50% more work every week. During those 5 hours there were no outside distractions, everyone was heads-down working and being very productive. It also allowed people to work without looking at the clock so often.

I found the 45 hours to be more energizing than draining. It built strong bonds each other, and forced us to do work that we were very proud of. More important, it enabled the company to pay a salary that excited us.

If you can get into a job where you enjoy the work, where you work hard, and where you receive good pay and good raises—it will create a reinforcing cycle of better performance and better pay. Both you and the company will help each other grow and get rich.

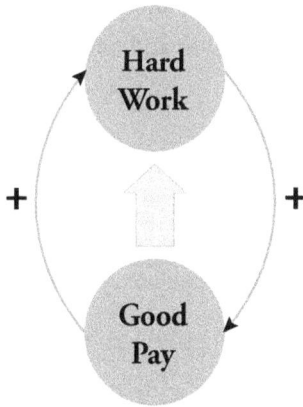

But if you get into a situation where you are disappointed in the job, you will do mediocre work, and receive mediocre pay. This is also a reinforcing cycle—but it reinforces all of the wrong things. You become more mediocre and more disappointed. The company becomes more mediocre and less competitive. As a result, they cannot pay you better to perform better. Eventually they will not be able to earn enough money to pay anyone anything. Eventually this cycle will lead to layoffs and company failure.

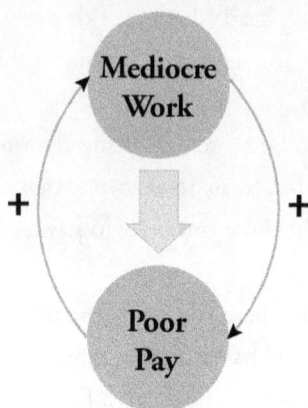

If you get stuck in the latter cycle you need to "pull chocks", "jump ship", "bail out", "hit the road", "pursue alternative options", "find greener pastures". In a word, you need to Quit and find someplace better.

Quitting

Quitting is part of success. It is part of getting ahead. When you get into a job and a company that creates the positive cycle we described above—stay, enjoy it, maximize it. But when you are spiraling down and things are getting worse—leave, quickly.

I have worked in many companies and generally I stayed in a bad situation too long. I was too lazy, too scared, or fooled into thinking it would get better. It never got better. It just got worse. When I did finally move on, I always found that I had made the right choice, even though I had waited longer than I should have.

Quitting and moving someplace else will open up new doors. It will show you challenges that you have never faced before. It will demand courage and confidence. It will be terrifying and thrilling.

It will also be financially rewarding. I told you that my move to Washington DC came with a 40% pay raise. Part of that was due to a more expensive living area. But a big part was due to market inflation.

When you are inside of a company the average raise falls around 3%, or maybe 4%. Every year most people get a 3% raise.

The bottom tier gets 0% or 1%.

The people in the middle gets 3 or 4%.

The people at the top gets 5, 6, or 7%.

And there are always a couple of superstars who get 10% or more.

So even if you are fluctuating between the middle and the top, you are getting between 3 and 7% each year. Every company has a hard year now and then and explains to everyone why raises just can't be very good this year—but they promise to make it up next year when times are better.

But they never do make it up.

While this is happening inside the company, the market demand for talent coming in from the outside is going up. In general it goes up around 5% per year. That means that over a 5 year period, the salaries inside the company have gone up by 15%. But the starting salaries for new talent out of college has gone up 25%.

It is common to discover that a new hire with less experience has a higher salary than someone who has been with the company and in a similar job for 10 years.

Sounds unfair doesn't it? The market system isn't fair. It is based on supply and demand. When the company needs more people it has to pay what the market demands. But the people who sit inside the company are not making any demands at all. They just accept what they are given.

Quitting and moving to a new company gives you the opportunity to tap into that market growth. It allows you to step up to the new standard of pay. It allows you to become the "new guy" who is making more than the people who have been there for years. It allows you to go from earning enough to be barely satisfied, to earning enough to be excited about going to work. It can move you into that positive cycle we talked about earlier.

So, are you brave enough to do it? Most people are not. They accept less. They fall behind.

Clean Slate

Quitting also gives you a clean slate at your new company. Everyone has a history after a few years on the job. You are stereotyped based on what you have done since day one. You might be known for being argumentative with coworkers. You may not get along with your boss. Everyone might remember the time you got drunk at the Christmas party and really went too far.

These events and images stick with you for years. Moving to a new company can erase all of these and give you a chance to try again. They let you learn from your mistakes. They let you leave you mistakes behind and start writing on a clean slate. This time you write a better story. You write the good story right from the very beginning.

Some of the stereotypes and barriers that are built up over the years are in your own head. You set yourself in a specific role, or at a specific spot on the totem pole. You see yourself at one place and you do not let yourself move forward. You become your own barrier to moving forward.

Changing jobs can break the mental chains that you have put on yourself.

Every company or organization is not the same. Moving across companies will give you exposure to new ways of looking at things. New ways to solve problems. New types of relationships. New working standards. If a competitor is beating the stuffing out of your company, there is a reason for that. They are doing something different. They have some advantage that your company is lacking. What is it? Going to work for them is one way to learn about new and different ways. It is one way to get off of the losing team and onto the winning team.

Fired

Getting fired will also move you along. It may be a little shocking. It may hurt your feelings or damage your pride. But millions of people get fired every year. It doesn't kill them. It challenges them to be stronger and to try something new and different.

Tom Peters was a big shot at McKenzie & Company, one of the world's leading business consulting companies. He got fired. He says it was the best thing that ever happened to him. It forced him to build his own company on the ideas he was researching and teaching. It forced him to grow into a huge management consultant of his own. It forced him to create The Tom Peters Company. It put him in a position to write a dozen books, speak at hundreds of meetings, and make millions of dollars.

Getting fired is not always a bad thing.

Most people who have been fired recover just fine. In fact, it is common for them to find better jobs with better future prospects than they had at their old jobs.

If you do get fired, just don't wither and die. Examine your work habits and ask whether it was due to something you were doing wrong. If it was, then fix that. But if the firing was part of a larger layoff driven by changes in the market or something outside of your control, then just shrug it off. Move on. There is something better up ahead for you.

I am speaking from experience. I was fired from a great position. I was in a company that missed a major shift in the market. They were losing business to competitors and just could not recover. If I had been paying attention I would have figured out a year earlier that it was time for me to leave. But I could not see that clearly. I kept thinking that things were going to turn around … somehow. I was working to get new business … but I wasn't succeeding. The teams that I was on were losing bids on several very big jobs. Hmmm? How long can that go on? Get a clue. The roof is about to cave in. Are you ready?

One day I heard through the grapevine that six other people in the same senior position that I had were laid off. I could see the ax coming. So I called my boss and asked what was happening. He said I should lay low and hope the higher executives didn't notice me. I said I was ready to take the layoff and the severance package. I would be fine.

By the time they did all the paperwork, gave the formal notice, and set the date for my departure I already had another job lined up. I moved into a smaller and very aggressive company with great benefits and an unbelievable culture for performance.

Quitting and getting Fired are all part of your professional life. Don't fear them. Use them to your advantage.

Work For Yourself

You have a job with a company and they have an agreement with you. The agreement is something like this—you do what we want and we will pay you a salary. There is some expectation that for that salary you will work at least 40, 50, or 60 hours per week.

So you go to work where they tell you and you do what they tell you. At first you're overwhelmed with new ideas and new information. You are struggling to figure everything out.

Eventually you will climb on top of the pile of work. Eventually you will have the time, energy, and knowledge to look around and think about what you see. Eventually you will be able to understand what is happening—whether it is good or bad—how you can contribute to it—and you will see your future. You will see what this company will do for you and to you if you stay for 5, 10, or 20 years. As you look at this you need to understand that you **can** have a huge say in what this future looks like. Or you can choose to have a tiny voice in it. You can accept what some system has in store for you. Or you can think, plan, and take action above, beyond, and across the system.

Wherever you are, you need to understand that you work for yourself. You get a paycheck from some other organization. But so does every person. None of us write ourselves a paycheck. We all make money by providing services to someone else. We create something of value to someone else.

We are all self employer. We all have a responsibility to think, plan, act, and be the person that we think is best. Not the person that the corporation maps out for us. When those two overlap, that is great. But when you have bigger dreams than the company does, you need to keep pursuing them. You need to be who you are, not who a manual says you will be.

I have seen a number of corporate operations manuals. They are usually very outdated. The person they describe is out of the 1980's or earlier. It is just not you. It is usually not anyone real. Also, I have never seen a company manual that shows the employee how to become a millionaire at this job. I have been in a number of jobs that did lead people to becoming millionaires. But the manual never mentioned anything about that. People were doing it on their own, the company manual was not providing much guidance on their path.

You always work for yourself at the same time that you work for a larger company. Don't forget to do the things that are important for your future, not just the things that are urgent for the company.

Where Are The Jobs

Everyone comes out of school like a mole coming out of the ground. They squint at the bright lights, are confused by all the bustling about, and try not to get run over by the real world. College may teach you a lot about engineering, teaching, and accounting. But it just never teaches you enough about … Where to get a job?

I teach seminars all over the country, so the employment picture is different every place I go. But there are a few constants. Every area is known for some kind of business. Silicon Valley is known for computers and chips.

San Francisco is known for the web and software. Hollywood is known for movies and computer games. Orlando is known for theme parks and resorts. This reputation is really a measure of how many jobs that city has in specific fields.

When you come out of college in a specific city, does your area of study match the kind of work that your town is known for? Yes? Then you are starting with an advantage. No? Then you are probably planning to move, right?

If you watch the local newspaper, you will find that every year they put out a list of the largest employers in the town. The largest does not mean the best. But it does mean something important. It does mean that you can get a job there when you are hungry. You might be surprised to learn who the largest employers are in your area. There are three that are always at the top in any geographic area:

1) The Government. State, County, and Federal
2) The Hospital System.
3) The Grocery Store Chain.

Many of these jobs are not professional, but they require an organizational hierarchy in which college graduates are doing the administration, management, and specialized jobs. They are a rich source of opportunities simply because there are so many jobs to keep filled.

So in addition to the companies or industries that are best known in your area, be sure to look into government, hospital, and grocery opportunities.

Take a few minutes to complete the Earning worksheets in the back of the book.

Baby Boomers

Have you heard that beginning salaries are not growing with the costs of goods and homes?

Have you heard that this generation does not have the opportunities to get ahead that their parents had?

Have you heard that you will not be able to afford a house or college or something else that your family provided to you?

If you have heard these, has anyone explained why this is happening in plain language that you understand?

I am going to give you 2 of the major causes of this situation. Why beginning salaries are so low. And why you cannot afford a house right now.

1) Baby Boom Generation
2) Credit Cards

We will cover credit cards in more detail in a later chapter. But right now I want to enlighten you on the effect that the baby boomers are having on your opportunities.

The Baby Boomers were born between 1945 and 1960. They are currently between 50 and 65 years old. They have had a career in most of the companies that dominate the world economy right now. They are the senior people in the senior jobs in those companies. They have the higher salaries. They have the biggest benefits packages. They use a lot of insurance.

The Baby Boomers are consuming a large and disproportionate percentage of the money that companies earn. There are a lot of them, they have the biggest pay packages, they have the senior jobs. Paying and sustaining them costs a lot of money. Companies are putting a lot of their revenue and profits into these people and they do not have much left for the new hires just coming out of college.

It was not always like that. There was a time when these big companies had a very small core of senior people. Perhaps 75% less than they have now. At that time they had the free revenue to pay more to new hires. Your opportunities, your paycheck are being squeezed by the Baby Boom generation.

In 5 to 15 years these people will be retiring. They will vacate the senior jobs that you want. They will release a salary that is large enough to hire 3 or 4 people like you. When that finally happens we will be back to the level of demand that existed after World War II.

The Baby Boomers also drive up the prices of goods because they can afford high prices on cars and homes. Houses are too expensive for you because you are competing to buy them against people who earn three or four times more than you do. They drive up the prices because they are still buying. When they stop earning and stop buying, prices will fall—especially on homes and cars. Real estate is not going to recover—there is too much supply from overbuilding in the last 10 years. There will soon be fewer buyers as the Baby Boomers retire. They will need senior housing, medicine, entertainment, travel, and "old people" cars. They will not need new homes. Demand for homes will drop to a level proportionate to the "Echo Boom". That is the children of the Baby Boomers. These people were born between 1970 and 1985. There are a lot less of them than there are of their parents.

Right now you are held back by the working Baby Boomers. In a few years, opportunity and money will be freed up and you will find a new job, promotion, and a raise much easier to get.

Walt Disney

Let's close the Earning session on a positive note. When you go to work take the advice of Walt Disney, *"Do what you do so well that they will want to see it again and bring their friends."*

That advice is custom fit to the theme park business. But you can do what you do so well, that your boss will want to see you do it again. You can do it so well that he will want to show his boss. You can do it so well that the entire company will want to be sure that you are doing it for them, not for their competitors.

Do what you do so well that your boss will want to see it again.

Rule 3:

Spend

How can a seminar on getting rich tell you to spend money? You are probably already an expert at that! Most of us have been practicing spending money ever since we were five years old. You say, *"Well at least I have one valuable talent ... and that is shopping. I can shop, I can spend, I can bring home the loot."*

You know that is exactly what corporate America hopes you will do. They spend billions of dollars every year explaining to you that you need to buy their stuff. They tell you on television, on the radio, on the internet, on billboards, in the newspaper, even on the walls in the restroom. They tell you, they sell you, they brainwash you. They make every product look like something amazing that will give you huge smiles and lots of pretty friends. You have noticed that all advertising emphasizes smiles and friends haven't you?

So corporate America turns on the advertising machine and you turn on the spending machine ... and everything is good. Right? You can afford to buy everything they are advertising can't you? You don't have to hold back. You have the money. Or you have the credit card. Buying all of that stuff is going to work out great. You will be happy. You will have friends. And you will have all that stuff.

But what won't you have? That's right, you won't have any money. You won't have any for the things you need. You won't build up any wealth. You won't have any money to pay your credit cards. You will never become a Millionaire Employee. Uh oh. That did not turn out so well did it?

There is simply **way** too much stuff in the world for anyone to buy all of it ... though many of us are trying our best to do it. So when do you stop? How do you decide when enough is enough? You can take you cue from the corporate advertising world. They say you don't have to stop until you have spent absolutely every penny you have earned, every penny you have saved, and every penny you can borrow on credit. Yep, that's the budge that they have for you. That is the position they **want** to put you in. That is what they spend billions of dollars a year to make happen.

When you pit your hand-me-down financial knowledge against a billion dollar advertising machine, who do you think is going to win? We already know the answer. Look around at your friends, parents, and professors. They all lost the fight. You are going to lose the fight ... unless you learn a better way to handle your money. Unless you find some bigger goals in life than buying more stuff.

In the Quick Start worksheet at the back of this book you can list all of the monthly and yearly bills that you have. This will help you identify where your money is going. It is basic and simple. Take some time and go through the spending worksheet.

Did you know that most people **never** do something as simple as that worksheet? Did you know that most people have no idea where their money goes? Sure they remember writing the big checks for rent, mortgage, insurance, and electricity. But they get paid a lot more than those checks, but somehow their money is always gone before they get to the next payday. Where did it go? They have no idea.

When you filled out the Quick Start worksheet you were probably a little, or a lot, surprised to see what some of your spending habits were. I know I was the first time I did it. In fact, I do this every year and am still surprised at some of the expenses that sneak in and suck out my money.

The **most** important part of spending money is knowing what you are spending it on. That is why it is part of the worksheet. If you don't know what you are doing, then there is no way to do it smartly. Most people are sleep walking through their spending. They remember the last purchase, but back before that everything becomes very fuzzy.

Now you are expecting me to put you on a budget aren't you? Well not so fast. A budget that says *"you can't do this"* and *"you can't do that"* is not going to work. It is far to negative. You need a plan that says what you **can** do and what you **want** to do.

America and the World have been incredibly productive and successful through the Industrial and the Information Ages. There was a time when you could not afford basic necessities—not because they were so rare and you were so poor. But because they were so difficult to make. Very few people had the skills to make the goods. Then there were so few ways to ship them to the world market. During the Industrial Age we learned to overcome the scarcity of goods. We learned about mass production and manufacturing. We figured out how to make thousands or millions of items very efficiently.

During the Information Age we figured out how to ship those goods efficiently to the people who could buy them. We learned to eliminate the waste from sending the wrong products to the wrong places. We eliminated the shortage of goods. Today there is no shortage of any product. Neither are there products that you cannot get anyplace in the modern world. We have conquered the production problem and the delivery problem.

What does that mean to you? It means that the world can deliver every product to you efficiently and cheaply. The industrial and information factories of the world can make anything at a very affordable price. They can ship it to your neighborhood Wal-Mart, Best Buy, and grocery store in numbers sufficient to meet all demand. It means that you have the ability to go out and buy **anything you need** and almost everything you want.

Your parents and their parents could not do this. Those goods were just not in the stores around them. In fact, the store itself was not there because there were no goods to put in it. In some cases the product was available, but the price was extremely high because of waste in the delivery system.

Today that has all changed. Today you can get almost anything somewhere near you. And certainly you can get it on the Internet if it is not within a short driving distance.

Why is that important?

It is important because there are literally so many goods out there in easy reach that **no one** can afford to buy all of them. But the marketing machine and society in general has been pushing us to try.

The reason you have more debt than you parents is that there are 1000 times more products around you than were around them at your age. Those products are also 10 times less expensive than they were to your parents. Each individual product looks very affordable. But all of them together are way beyond your means.

You need to learn something that your parents did not need to learn. You need to understand that goods are so plentiful that **no one** can buy all of them. Not even Bill Gates, though he might come close.

You are rich enough to buy everything that you **need**. You can afford to buy something everywhere you go. But you cannot afford it all.

You need some boundaries on how much you let yourself acquire. Because there is no limit to how much the marketplace can deliver to you.

There are an infinite number of things to buy.

No one can afford all of them.

You can afford some of them.

When do you stop?

The key to knowing when to stop, how much to spend, how far to go is .... PAY YOURSELF FIRST. Then you will know what you can afford.

This is the most important thing you are going to learn in this book. You are going to hear a little right now and a lot more in the next chapter.

A budget means knowing how much you can spend on yourself. It does not mean starving yourself for the rest of your life. It means setting your lifestyle at a level where you can enjoy the present and become rich in the future. Everyone tries to set this level too high.

Imagine that you are snorkeling in the ocean. Have you ever been snorkeling? If you have, then you know that you see the fish in the water around you and you might be able to see the bottom below you. In the Florida Keys there are lots of snorkeling spots where the bottom is just 15 or 20 feet down. In the Keys, if you want to, you can explore every inch of the ocean from the surface all the way to the bottom. But if you move off-shore just a mile you will find the bottom drops away and it might be 100 feet or 1,000 feet to the bottom. At this point it is impossible for you to snorkel to the bottom. You can still explore the top 15 or 20 feet. But the rest is out of your range. Stop trying to go to 25 or 30 feet. The water and the fish down there are the same as those in the top 10 to 15 feet.

The world of spending is like that. You need to learn that everything you need is in that top 10 to 15 feet. Everything deeper than that is exactly like what you see around you. Stop trying to get at all of it.

Be amazed, happy, and blessed with what you have within your reach and your current income. You can already afford more than 90% of the people alive on the planet. When will you have enough stuff? You do not need more stuff to be happy. What you need is control over your situation. You need to be free from the stress, worry, and misery that comes from being deeply in debt and seeing no way out. You need to give up the things that are making you miserable and treasure the things you can afford. You need to learn to be thankful for the rich life you can enjoy now.

Let your income support both your current needs and joys—**and** you future needs and joys. That will eliminate the stress and worry. That will make your inner mental and spiritual life richer than your already extremely rich outer life.

You can choose where you spend your money. But to choose you have to understand where the money is going. A budget is more about knowing where your money is going than it is about holding back. It creates an objective picture so you can have a conversation with yourself about what you are doing. Without it, the flow of money is just a fuzzy idea in the dark alleys of your brain. Nothing is really clear and you can't really take action on it because you can't see it clearly

Where Does It Go

When you start keeping track of where you spend your money, you are going to find that the big money-eaters are generally the same for everyone. The Big Expenses are:

1) **Taxes, Social Security, and Medicaid** taken directly out of your check. These come in and take a big chunk of your money before you ever see it. If you watch these every check you will get depressed. We all do. Especially when you need money for bills and you can see that something like 25% of your check just disappeared. You cannot do anything about Social Security and Medicaid. But you can do something about Taxes. We will address that later in the Incorporate chapter.

2) **Your Home**, either in the form of rent or a mortgage payment. This is also boosted up by the cost of maintaining that home. Electricity, water, repairs, and lawn care all add to the price of living in a home. Then we buy furniture, pictures, carpet, trash cans, towels, and a million other things that fill up that space we live in.

3) **Cars**. Your primary car and for some of you your second hobby car. This also includes your boat, jet ski, motorcycle, or RV. Just like your home, these all call for care and feeding. Filling the gas tank, general maintenance, repairs, insurance, washing and cleaning, and all the trinkets that you like to keep inside.

4) **College tuition, books, fees, and supplies**. For many of you college will become a part of your life for years to come. You will be on-and-off students and studiers at a college much longer than previous generations. Remember that in the Learn chapter I recommended getting a Master's degree. I know that was a painful piece of advice for some of you. But you don't have to start on that immediately after the Bachelor's degree. You can enjoy your first degree and the boost it gives to your brain and wallet for a few years before tackling another degree.

5) **Credit Cards**. People say we have transitioned from the Industrial Age to the Information Age. I think it is just as accurate to say that we have transitioned from the Cash Age to the Credit Age. Try to imagine a time when people did not use credit cards. They paid for everything with cash and a few things with checks. There was always immediate cash backing up every purchase. You think, *"wow that must have been a century ago."* No, it was just about 20 years ago. The madness of holding 5, 10, or 20 credit cards and having

a balance to pay on all of them is relatively new. There was a time when the monthly bills **did not** include paying toward a credit card balance. Today we all spend more than we make by using credit cards. We do this every month, but somehow imagine a time when we will pay them off. That is a fantasy world for 90% of the people who are doing using them.

6) **Insurance**. Auto, home, life, medical, dental, liability, hospital payment, accidental death, and property insurance. There are literally dozens to hundreds of forms of insurance available. What is insurance? It is protection against the things that you cannot afford to have happen to you. It protects you from the cost of disasters that would wipe you out financially. It is not good to have insurance on things that are no big deal and that you can afford to handle yourself. The extended warranty that you buy on a new camera or computer is not necessary. It is a huge profit item for the store and just more debt for you.

7) **Travel.** Some people travel to their family and back. Some travel to Las Vegas and back. Some travel to Europe and back. All of this adds up to an expense riding on your credit card.

8) **Clothing.** Do you know how many pieces of clothing you wear at one time? Most people wear between 6 and 10 items at once. Some of us wear a few more. Given styles and different social settings, you might have 12 to 24 to 100 different outfits. This can come to 1,000 pieces of clothing. If you wear these out, then you must be replacing these 1,000 items every year or two. That is a big rotation of goods.Clothing is a key area where there are literally a thousand times more items than we can possibly afford.

9) **Electronics**. Electronics have replaced the automobile as a primary area of spending. Everyone needs a television, DVD player, game console, computer, cell phone, iPod, portable DVD player, another iPod, memory sticks, and other digital do-dads. This can really add up. Usually it adds up on your credit card.

10) **Medical**. In a young audience most people are lucky enough that they have no major medical expenses. You might spend a small amount on cold medicines, an occasional doctor's visit, and a trip to the dentist. But you do not have the crushing medical bills that settle in on people as they get older. In an older audience, medical expenses can become the number one expense on the list. It is impossible to get rich under the constant care of a doctor and the medical profession. Good health is a primary ingredient for becoming rich. It can allow you to escape from thousands of dollars of expenses every year and hundreds of thousands over a lifetime.

David And Goliath

Once you start to see and understand your spending you are going to find out that there are a number of Goliaths in your life that have more control, more ownership, and more say in what you do than you do.

These Goliaths are:

- Large Corporations,
- Madison Avenue,
- Wall Street, and
- the Government.

That makes four big giants—against you. All of them control more of your personal wealth than you do. They also work extremely hard to convince you to do what is good for them. Even when it is not good for you.

What is good for them? Spending.

What is good for you? Saving and Investing.

Compare the amount of money you put into these two big categories—spending and saving. Which is larger? We already know. You **have** to spend more than you save. But you **do not** have to spend more than you make. Most of you are spending more than you make. Most of you are controlled by the Goliaths.

Imagine a world in which you work for Goliath Great Buy. They pay you $200/week. Your friend works as Goliath Bullseye and also earns $200/week. Bullseye and Great Buy work toward the same goal. They hire Madison Avenue to help them get their message across. They both want you to spend everything you make and then borrow more on your credit card to go further.

If they succeed, then they pay you $200. But you spend $220. That means that they get back more money than they gave you. You do all of the work, but you spend more than you make from them. So at the end of the week they each have $20 more than they started with and you are $20 more in debt.

How does this turn out over the long run? It turns out that you work for nothing. In fact, you work for negative pay because you push $20 worth of debt into your own future. But the Goliaths get all of that money right now. They are not just making normal profits by competing against each other. They are making super profits by also convincing you to go into permanent debt. They have convinced you to carry the burden of the economy on your shoulders and to earn nothing for carrying that burden.

This is a great system … for the Goliaths. This is what has been happening for the last several years. This is why you see so many "get out of debt" companies advertising on TV. This is why the "We Buy Your Gold" companies are sprouting up everywhere. The Goliaths have convinced the Davids that owning more stuff and getting impossibly deep into debt is a great idea.

It is not a great idea. It has put people so deep in debt that they are now desperate to find a way out. These Gold and Debt companies are convincing people to spend even more money to find a way out of debt. Be careful in working with them, their goal is also to get more of your money.

The economic model where you earn $200 and spend $220 has to change if you are going to be wealthy. You have to replace it with the earn $200 and spend $180 model. You have to oppose the tyrannical rule of the Goliaths and make your own decisions.

I am sorry to say that even the politicians are on the Goliaths side. In fact they are one of the Goliaths. What has the national message been ever since 9/11? It has been, *"Keep shopping!"—"America is not in danger. Your jobs are safe. The economy is safe. Just keep shopping!"*

The financial crisis is not a surprise. How it happened is no mystery. The shopping society reached its limits. The "Earn 200, Spend 220" model went as far as it could go. Eventually people had to pay up or crumble. They are crumbling. And the companies that lent David money are also crumbling.

The economy has been over heated by over shopping. Now we will cool down during a period of under shopping. It is going to be painful. It is going to be prolonged—like 5 years. But everything is going to be OK.

The best thing you can do for yourself is adopt the model of "Earn 200, Spend 180". Or if you already have big debt—Earn 200, Spend 180, Payoff 20.

That is **not** good for Goliath. But it **is** good for David. You are David.

Choices

We all have to pay taxes, rent, mortgage, electricity, gasoline, maybe a car payment, and a few others. But after that we choose to create the bills we have.

We all have free time. We all have entertainment and hobbies that fill that time. What are your hobbies and entertainments? Your choices have a lot to do with where your money goes. Your choices make a big difference in the size of your credit card bills.

Maybe you love sports, running, basketball, or soccer.

Maybe you are into movies or reading books.

Maybe you just like to party and meet people.

Maybe you are a crafter who makes things.

Maybe you work on cars or electronics for fun.

Or maybe your hobby is just spending money.

If your entertainment, your source of relaxation and enjoyment is shopping, then you are probably already in trouble.

How long does it take to buy a new pair of pants? Just one pair? 30 minutes? 10 minutes?

At your job, how much do you earn in 30 minutes? At minimum wage it would be around $3. At $25,000/year it would be around $6.50. At $50,000 it is $13. Those are all before taxes. After taxes the numbers are like $2, $5, and $10.

How much does that pair of pants cost? I'll bet it is more than $10. It might be $20 at the least, or more likely over $50.

You cannot earn $10 in 30 minutes and have a hobby where you spend $50 in 30 minutes. You can see that you just have to shop for 8 hours/week to spend every penny you bring home. That is a little over one hour of shopping per day.

Shopping and Eating Out are two of the worst hobbies or forms of entertainment. They are great luxuries. But they are terrible hobbies.

You need hobbies that cost less per hour than you earn per hour. We did not even factor in all of the real expenses you have before figuring this out. If your bills consume 80% of your income. Then you earn $10 every 30 minutes, you spend $8 of that on your core necessities, and you only have $2 left to use for entertainment.

Your budget is $2 per 30 minutes. But you are spending $50 in 30 minutes to buy a pair of pants. Maybe you just spend $15 in 30 minutes for a pair of pants at a discount store.

You need a different kind of hobby that you enjoy and that will consume your time and your energy.

Two of the Best are Learning and Physical Activity.

Learning can be going to school in the evenings, taking seminars, reading books, or watching educational television and movies. I have a couple of favorite places to get an education on my own:

- Half.com where I can get books at bargain prices. I read a lot of books and save thousands of dollars every year by getting them used instead of new.

- Wikipedia where I can read up on almost any topic for free. I can also write articles in my areas of expertise.

- Netflix where I can get some great videos from Suze Orman and others. I can also see all the movies I "should" see, those that are good for my social education and view of the world.

- Audible.com where I get audio books to keep me busy while driving to work, driving between seminars, and working out. This lets me "read" books that I would never get to in paper form. They also have a great selection of financial and career management books.

Physical activity is one hobby that gets you out of the office and up off of the couch. It gets your blood pumping, changes your surroundings, and puts you around other people. If you look at your body you will notice that your head, brain, eyes, and ears are just 10% of the package. The other 90% is below your neck. What are you doing with that 90%? Most of us do not and will not have jobs that make a lot of use of that 90% of our bodies. Office jobs focus on your brain and your hands. You think and communicate. So it makes sense that we use our free time to put our bodies to work or put them into play.

You might choose running, working out at a gym, bicycling, basketball, yoga, or swimming. You might prefer fixing cars, planting a garden, or building something with your hands.

All of these break the mental obsession and the stress that comes from your working day. You can pour your problems out on the road, in the gym, or under the hood of a car. The tension and the jumbled thinking come out almost like they are part of the sweat you are losing.

All of these require an investment. You need gear, tools, or memberships. It is important that you spend less at this activity than you earn. Try the spend-per-hour vs. earn-per-hour comparison on these expenses to make sure you are not just finding another way to go broke. The goal is not to buy more stuff to be active—it is to be active so you spend less time buying stuff.

Financial Crisis–Again

Listen to the messages about the financial crisis. What are they? One of the major messages is, *"Get the consumer back to spending. Make credit easy to get so people can buy a house or continue shopping."* Too much shopping is what got us into the mess in the first place. People who had no ability to repay their loans were given loans for a house or credit cards for shopping. On Wall Street they repackaged and resold those loans—made their billions—and just tried not to be the one holding the bag when the music stopped.

The kind of shopping and spending that has been happening for the last 5 to 10 years is abnormal. It put us all in debt way over our heads. Listen to the radio or television commercials. There are two new kinds of ads that did not used to exist. The first are the Debt Consolidation ads. There are so many people in trouble that these companies are multiplying like rabbits. The second are the "We Buy Your Gold" companies. These are just a new form of pawn shop. They are taking advantage of your financial distress. They are prepared to buy your gold at a fraction of what it is worth because they know you are desperate to find more money.

Five or ten years ago, these companies were rare. And they certainly could not afford the prime time advertising they are doing now. But the crushing debt that people have has made these companies much more profitable and given them the opportunity to take your valuables at a fraction of what they are worth.

We all have to control our spending. We all have to live within our means … again. It is not rare. It is not impossible. It has been done for centuries. We are going to go back to it one way or another—by choice or by the force of poverty.

You must start saving 10%, put it into something that brings a return to you. You must stay out of credit card debt. This denies the Goliaths the power to enslave you in debt. It demands that the corporate machine shoulder some of the burden for running society. It requires that they take out loans to run their business and pay interest—instead of forcing that debt onto your shoulders.

If you are willing to ratchet up your spending to 110% of your income, then there is no reason for any company to give its employees a raise. The people will spend more and the companies will make more, but without having to pass the wealth on to the people who work for them. They earn more by giving you debt instead of a raise. Your pay raise is converted into credit card debt. The big system approves of more credit for you, but not more pay.

> How many of you have an iPod?
> How many have two iPods?
> How about three?

> How many of you have a cell phone?
> How many have two working cell phones?
> How many have three?

Did you buy these with cash or credit? Are they paid off or still riding on that credit card?

Two cell phones is an example of your over spending. Keeping the cost on your credit card is an example of you carrying too much debt. Together these kinds of activities are going to make you poor and keep you poor.

Credit Card Addicts

In America most people are Credit Addicts. This is just like a drug addict. The symptoms are the same—you think about shopping all the time, you use your credit card at least once a day, you cannot imagine a life without credit, you get violent if someone tries to take your credit card away.

Today, most people get addicted to credit in college. The credit card companies or major retailers approve a card for you. Maybe they entice you by getting you to open an account just to buy one single item, like a new television. Then you start using it casually. Pretty soon you find that you need a little more. You open another account or make more frequent use of an account you already have. If you are lucky your income is also rising so you keep this war between debt and income going for several years. But have you ever completely paid off all of your credit card debt? Have you ever received a statement with the magic balance of $0 on it?

Most people get into debt while in college, and never get out for the rest of their lives. It's a lifelong habit that they never break.

This debt will cause personal and relationship stress for your entire life.

This debt will stop you from becoming wealthy because you are paying 18% more for every item—that is 18% more for every year that the bills ride on your credit card.

There is no way to be frugal enough in other areas to make up for the 18% interest on all charged purchases.

Paying off credit card debt and learning to control your spending is the #1 thing you must do to become wealthy. If you don't, it will destroy all of your efforts to get ahead by making more at your job. You can always spend more than you can make, no matter how big your salary is.

Credit Cards

Learning The Hard Way

My mother has been going to the same hairdresser for 20 years. This lady has owned that business for 31 years. She has many loyal customers like my mother and is well known in town. However, she confided to my mom that in 31 years she has never managed to save a single dollar. She has worked hard and created a successful business. But she has also spent every penny that came in the door. She is now in her sixties and realizes that she cannot run this shop forever. She is looking at her very near future and realizing that she needs some savings. She can see the end of her working life coming up fast and she will have nothing but Social Security to live on.

Her Social Security will be somewhere between $500 and $1,200 per month. She is looking at a future of living on $6,000 to $14,000 a year. Given where she is right now, that future is almost certain. There are very few options for her to make a significant change this late in her life.

Everyone comes to this realization sometime in their life. But not everyone figures it out in time to do something about it. If you are reading this, it is time to start doing something about it now. You are going to build lifetime wealth, not lifetime debt.

Spending Challenge #1

If you have a spending problem—if you have more credit card debt than you should, then I have a challenge for you. Stop using your credit cards for one month. Don't buy anything that you can't pay for with cash or your ATM card (without triggering a backup Line of Credit).

Just for one month live within your means. Live at your real income level.

Spending Challenge #2

The second challenge is to reduce your credit card debt. Get your bill from last month. Add up all of the charges you put on the card that month. Was it

$100, $200, $500? Whatever it was, during your NO CHARGING month I want you to make a payment on your credit card that is the same size as the amount you charged last month.

Ouch!

The first challenge was going to be hard enough. But some of you are thinking that the second one will be impossible.

Let me point out that the only way to be a Millionaire Employee is to get the Credit Card Goliath off of your back. You have to get those balances to ZERO. You want to find out what that will be like? Then stop adding to the balance and start subtracting from it. Stop Charging and Start Paying.

Pay as much per month as you used to charge per month. At that rate you will get out of debt almost as fast as you got into it. And you will get out ten times faster than if you are just paying the minimum required payment.

Spending Challenge #3

Now, can you ratchet that payment number up each month? Can you dig yourself out a little more each month than you dug yourself in?

Can you pay off the card in one year if you stop adding to it right now?

Your spending plan is to live within your means. That does not mean spending everything you make from here on out. It means spending less than you make and using the rest to pay off your credit cards.

Culture Current

There is a strong emotional current in society. It is like the current in a rushing stream. In a stream the current causes all of the fish to go in the same direction. They swim left and right, but the whole school of fish gradually moves in the direction of the current. Some fish move that direction very quickly, others meander. But they are all pushed by the current.

In modern society there is a cultural current at work on everyone. That current has four strong rules that catch everyone eventually.

1) spend all of your money,
2) borrow more via credit cards and spend all of that too,
3) take out a loan for your home and autos and pay it off as slowly as possible,
4) get in debt as soon as possible and stay there your entire life.

This is the direction that everyone goes. There is a lot of comfort in doing the same things that everyone else does. You may get into trouble, but it is comforting to talk to friends who are in the same boat. It is comforting to hear that your parents did the same thing. It is comforting to read about people who have the same problems that you have. At least if you drown, you will have lots of company at the bottom of the river.

This kind of cultural behavior is great for the Goliaths of the world.

1) Increases wealth for the corporations. The bankers, insurance companies, and retailers are all getting extremely rich off of your spending.

2) Increases government tax revenues. Federal, state, and local governments take in more taxes when you spend more money.

3) Crushing debt for the individual. You will accumulate a level of debt that you can never escape. It will hang over your life until you are dead.

Does this sound like a winning formula for you? Does it sound like a plan designed in your best interest? Does it sound like the path to your personal wealth? Does it sound like you becoming a Millionaire Employee?

No it does not.

Rule 4:

Save

I actually think that a plan for how you save your money is a **lot** more important than a budget. When you receive a paycheck you know what the **FIRST** thing you should do with the money is?

PARTY!

No, not exactly.

You need to pay the person who is going to be your partner for the rest of your life. You need to pay the person who has done all of the work to earn the money. You need to pay the person who is going to take care of you when you are young and when you are old. That sounds like your wife or husband doesn't it?

No, it is you.

Pay Yourself First

The first person you need to pay with that money is yourself. What does that mean? You think you already got paid when the check arrived or was deposited into your checking account. No, that is wrong. That is what everyone thinks. When you turn that money into cash or put it into a checking account it is not paid to you. You are just holding it for a few days or a few weeks while you pay it out to everyone else. There is always a long line of people waiting to get that money. Most of them are there because you put them in the line yourself. These are people like the waitress at the restaurant where you went to dinner, the cashier where you went to buy your new cell phone, or the phone company whom you gave your billing address so they would make your phone work every day. You put all of these people in a line to get your money.

Now look at that line. Do you see **yourself** anywhere in the line? Do you see Jamie or Joshua or Stephen or Pam standing there with a bill to be paid? No? Hmmm ... that is not good. So you work hard all month. You earn a good paycheck. Then you pay out all of it to your friends in retail. But the person who did all of the work to earn the money does not get any of the money themself? Does that sound right? Does that sound like the road to wealth? Does that sound like the way to become a Millionaire Employee?

In financial management circles the idea of putting yourself at the front of the pay-me line is called *"Paying Yourself First"*. There will always be lots of people in the line to get your money. There will always be more of them than you can pay off if you are not careful. You need to be in that line too. But you cannot be at the back of the line. The guy or girl at the back never gets paid. They always get the "maybe next month" story. You have to make sure that **you** are not the person at the back.

Put yourself at the front of this line. Pay yourself first. You do this by immediately, automatically, regularly, and religiously sending part of your pay
check to a savings account or an investment account. This account should
have only one door on it. That door is labeled "IN". It should not have an
"OUT" door … at least not right now. At the beginning of your career you
need to put money in and leave it there. Don't **ever** take the money out …
except when it is ready to be used for the Investment part of your plan.

Putting yourself at the front of the line is simple, but it is not easy. It is
simple because you can set-up automatic deposits into a savings or investment account. It takes a few minutes and one or two pieces of paper. But it
is not easy because the other people in line are going to yell, scream, cry, and
complain that you are not paying them first. Corporate America is going
to do everything they can to get you to stop that saving thing. They want
absolutely every single dollar you can get your hands on and every dollar
you can borrow. They have lots of money to spend on messages to convince
you to do that. You are going to feel the strong pull to pay them first and to
move yourself to the back of the line. Don't ever do it! Not ever! You always
stand in the front of the line.

Advertising in America is like the Adam and Eve story. It is a temptation
that does not ever go away. It is a temptation that comes at you all day every
day and never lets up. It always says … spend everything … save nothing …
then borrow more and spend that too. You are going to have to stop listen-
ing to that message and listen to advice that is good for you, not good for
Corporate America.

So how much of your pay **should** you save? Notice that I did not say how
much **can** you save. Everyone in America says, *"My bills are just too high. I
can't save anything. Just when I put a few dollars aside, there is an emergency*

and I have to spend that money." That is what everyone says. That is what everyone really believes too. But it is not true. It is a brainwashing job that has been done on you from the day you first turned on a television or radio right up until today. The brainwashing job says *"Spend it all! Then borrow more so you can spend more! You have to have more stuff."* Hogwash! Brainwash! Don't you believe it! You can save a **lot** more than you think you can.

Let me put a goal out there for you. This goal is aggressive. It is enough to help you really become wealthy. But it is also a lot less than some of you will be able to do. But it is big enough that you are going to have to un-brainwash yourself a little to reach it. The number is 10%. One thin dime out of every dollar you bring home.

Let's try an experiment. Open your wallet or purse right now. Count how much money is in there. Now take out 10% of that. If you have a $20 bill you need to take out two measly little dollars. If you have $100, then take out $10. You might have to get change to do this. But, don't buy something so you can have the change. Just ask a cashier for change.

Now take your 10% and put it away someplace in your house. Put it in the sock drawer. Put it in the cookie jar. Someplace that you will not look at it every day. And someplace so you are not carrying it with you wherever you go. Now just go about your business. Spend your money and see if you can get by without using that money. I'll bet you don't have any problem getting by without it. You might have to say, *"Oops, I took that money out of my wallet. I am not going to be able to buy that book ... or lunch ... or soda ... or whatever."* You will skip one of these things and it will be over. You will still have your 10%.

What if you did that for every dollar that went through your wallet? What if every time you bought something with your ATM card, you asked for 10% cash back and then put that money in your little savings nook? Try it for one month. You will start to get the feel for how big and how small 10% is. You will also get a good feel for how much control you have over your own spending.

The 1-2-3 Plan

Some of you are in a position where jumping to 10% immediately really is impossible. You need some time to work your way out of your existing financial obligations. For you I offer the 1-2-3 Plan. This month save just 1% of your income. That is one penny on every dollar. One dollar out of every hundred.

Next month save 2%. If you can, snag the entire 2% at the beginning of the month or from your first paycheck.

The month after that save 3%.

Raise it 1% every month. By the end of the year you will be at 12%. Go all the way to 12%, do not stop at 10%. That will let you makeup a little for the early months when you were saving 1%.

If you can reach 12% in one year, then you should have learned how to control your spending and how to pay yourself first. How will you proceed from there? Where will you take this? You can keep the number at 12%, dial back to 10%, or dial up to 15%. You decide what is possible.

Do What Is Hard

Can you do what is hard?

Saving is not easy. Controlling spending in our consumption mad society is not easy. If it were easy, then everyone would be doing it. Everyone would be building personal wealth. My seminars would not have anyone filling up all of those seats.

In your life you have already shown that you have the ability to do things that are hard. You are the kind of person who **can** do this if they put their will to it. What have you done that is hard? Maybe something from this list:

- Excelled at your school work
- Graduated High School
- Resisted Peer Pressure to do something you knew was wrong
- Put out the effort to excel at a sport
- Learned to play a musical instrument or to sing
- Supported a family through a crisis
- Endured a personal tragedy and emerged stronger

What is your hard thing? Where have you shown you are strong?

I speak to many new college graduates. That was a hard job for them. There are millions of people who could not get as far as those graduates did. Many people start college and give up after one semester, one year, or even one week. There are millions more who are afraid to take a swing at college. These people set themselves up in a job after high school and hope to make their fortune from there. Some of them will. You will meet some of them at your 10 year high school reunion. They may have taken over a family business, started their own business, gone into insurance, or worked in a com-mission-based field. They will have done as well as the college graduates.

But most of the people who refuse to tackle a college degree put a huge DEAD END sign in their immediate future. They are not going to do well. They are going to struggle financially and socially for their entire lives. They are always going to be dogged by those "unexpected" bills and emergencies that tap into everything they make … and more.

I have a tip for you … there are no "unexpected emergencies". We all face them. We all encounter them at some time. We are all surprised that it hap-pened to us. But some people are ready and others never get ready. You have these kinds of emergencies waiting for you in your future. The question is whether you will be prepared to handle them or whether they will seriously cripple your finances.

Janitor For Life

I want to tell you the story of a great guy who made one of these dead end decisions. I had a friend named James in high school who worked part-time as the janitor at the elementary school. The pay was pretty good … for a high school kid. He was making more than those of us working fast food or sacking groceries. After I graduated high school I got very busy with college and my first professional job. As a result I missed the 10 year class reunion. But when the 20 year reunion rolled around I was determined to get back and see what had happened to everyone.

I arrived at the reunion and most people were really great. It was good to see some of them again … and often surprising. I was particularly surprised at how many of them had stayed in that little down and made a nice life for themselves and their families. I turned around and there was James—always a really nice guy. I said, *"So James, what have you been up to?"* And he replied, *"Not much, just the same thing."* I said, *"Oh, well I missed the 10 year reunion, so I don't know what the same thing is."*

His reply struck me like a ton of bricks. He said, *"No the same thing as in high school. I am still the janitor at the elementary school."*

That janitorial job was a good opportunity for a high school kid. But it was not the kind of job you base your whole life on. It had a gigantic DEAD END sign on it and James had reached that END almost twenty years earlier.

James decided not to try to tackle anything hard. He decided at 18 that he couldn't handle any more than he had right then. He settled for what an 18 year old high school kid was capable of accomplishing.

You can not do that. You are still climbing. You are showing yourself that you can do things that are hard. Saving money is hard. But not trying is just sad. You can do this. You are smart enough. You are tough enough. You have shown that you are persistent enough.

There is a quote painted on the wall of the gym where I workout. It says, *"Don't let weakness convince you that you lack strength."*

You have strength. And you will develop more strength in your life. You are not done growing. You are not gone getting stronger—physically, mentally, emotionally, and spiritually. You can handle this. You can handle it very well.

Make A Trade

I want you take take a piece of paper and draw a line down the center from the top to the bottom. Label the left side "Current Spending". Label the right side "Future Spending". On the left side I want you to make a list of the things that you are doing right now with your money. These are the things that you think you have to do every day or every week because that is your habit, your personality, or your obligation. On the right side I want you to make a list of the things that you think you should be doing with your money that you are not doing. These are things that you know are good for you and necessary, but you do not have the time or have not put forward the effort to tackle yet.

What you see on the left is a short picture of who you are today in terms of spending. This is who you will be tomorrow and the next day as long as you keep spending on that list. What you see on the right side is a picture of who you want to be. It shows the kind of things you want to do in the future, sooner or later.

Making the first list on the left is easier if you have tracked your spending for a month. You can also use your ATM or credit card statement to help you make this list. Write down what you are buying and how much you paid for each item or service.

The second list contains the things you want to do with your money. These are the things that you know you should do, but are not doing. They are usually something you plan to get to in the future when you have more money or fewer bills. Be very generous with putting items on both lists. Don't hold back. Don't try to trick yourself into making this easy.

Now pick two items from the left side and two comparable items from the right side. Swap them. Make the current spending items, into future spending and the future spending items into current spending items. Decide right now that you **are** going to hold off on the things you are buying and you **are** going to use that money for just two things on your future spending list.

That is all—just two things.

You are not changing your whole life. You are just making two changes to the way you spend your money.

Both of these lists could be very long. That's a good thing. Long lists reveal more about your spending and they help you see that changing two items is really very small.

Most people's Future Spending list contains things like:

- Activate my 401(k)
- Max out my 401(K)
- Create an IRA account
- Create a savings account, or put in $100/month
- Find a good investment for my money
- Go back to college
- Give some money to a charity
- Increase my contribution at church

All of these are great ideas. We all know we want to do more of this ... but perhaps not right now. Switching two items on your list is a start toward making "someday" into "today". You can't change your life if you are not willing to put your foot down and decide that today is the day to get started.

Parents Teach Saving

Did you know that most of us were programmed in the first 10 years of our lives by the teachings and behaviors of our parents? We watched and absorbed like sponges. Their behavior determined where we went to school, what sports we pursued, which church we attended, what kind of people we dated, what kind of person we eventually married, and a hundred more behaviors that are core to who we are.

Our parents' behavior also has a lot to do with the way we treat money. It determines our attitude toward spending and saving, our level of risk in investments, and our inclination toward starting a business.

What did your parents teach you about saving money? I want you to pull those lessons out of the recesses of your brain. It is time to get out another piece of paper. Divide this one into four squares by making a line down the center and a line across the middle. Label each quadrant with the following:

- Parents' Wisdom
- College Lessons
- Television and Media
- On the Job

Now think back and try to remember incidences or specific lessons that you were given regarding saving money. What ideas were you given from each of these sources?

In these lists can you see the sources of your behaviors toward money and saving? Do you see that your ideas originated with your parents or from a specific course?

If you do not like the ideas you have about saving money you can change them. Many of the ideas are not your own to begin with. They were given to you by someone else. You adopted the wisdom or behavior of other people whom you thought knew better than you did. If you now understand that those ideas were not right, you can change them. You can choose to adopt anyone's ideas that you like. You can follow the ideas that help you, and abandon those that have not worked for you.

Keep Track

One of the problems with managing money and saving money is that there are so many ways to spend the money, but so few ways to earn it. It is easy to let money trickle out of the cracks in your life. Money is like water, it can leak through the smallest crack or hole. It may get out through automatic deductions from your paycheck. It may rush out through your ATM card, check book, or credit cards. It may escape via online shopping or the cash that walks out of your wallet.

It can be really difficult to get a handle on what is happening. You get so busy working and spending that you just don't have time to watch what is going on. But there are some really good services and tools available that will help you see what is happening. I recommend that you check out several online services to track your spending. Some of these are:

- Quicken Online
- Mint.com
- JustThrive.com

All of them are free to use. But they do ask you to provide your account numbers so they can pull together all of your spending and earning into one place. If you are going to use one, you need to find one that you trust with this kind of information. But you will see that they really can show you a picture of your spending and saving habits. It is a picture that is clear and scary at the same time.

This is just one tool in your battle with the Goliaths of corporate America. It will help you control who gets your money.

The Saving Bar

When you save money there are three basic places in your pay cycle that you can do it. You can save after you have paid your bills. You can save before you have paid your bills. You can save before you have paid your taxes. Each of these leads to a different amount of money, a different level of consistency, and a different final pool of wealth.

The Hope Method

When most people get paid they immediately see the money as a means to do two things—(1) enjoy themselves, and (2) pay their bills. These two things use up all of the money they have available. To become financially wealthy you have to see a third use for your money—(3) save to build wealth. If you are just getting started with your savings plan you probably have very little experience with how much you can put aside and will find it difficult to balance #1 fun and #2 bills now that you have crowded in the new #3 saving.

First time savers are afraid that they are going to hurt themselves by saving money. So they want to put off the saving until the end of the month or the end of the week. They like to pay their bills, go out to dinner, see a movie, and buy new shoes—then see how much is left over to save. As we have said earlier, there are more shoes, clothes, electronics, restaurants, and movies than any one person can buy. So this is going to be a tough fight.

Under the Hope Method your spending looks something like the bar graph below with Taxes first, Expenses second, Luxuries third, and Saving fourth. Where is saving in this picture? It is at the end of the line. Does the person at the end every get paid? No.

Hope Method

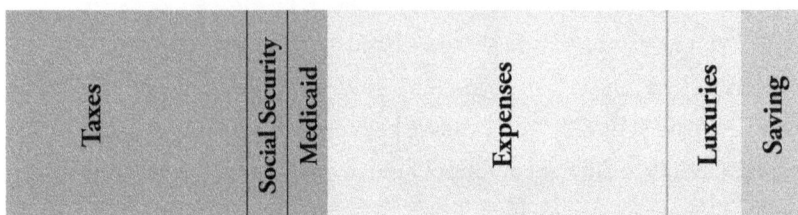

This method is the hardest because there are just too many other things demanding attention. It will struggle along and generate different levels of saving every month. You might have to save this way for one or two months just to get in the habit. You might do this while you are opening the savings or investment accounts you are going to need to save money. But you can't stick with this method very long. You need to move on to something more successful.

The Smart Method

A much smarter way to save the 10% you are targeting is to pay yourself first. You have to have a separate savings account at a bank or an investment account with a brokerage company. Opening one is identical to opening a checking account. You are going to transfer money from your paycheck directly into your savings account. Many employers offer direct deposit services. That means they will send your paycheck directly to your checking account rather than giving you a paper check to cash.

If they have this service, they may also allow you to split your check and direct deposit into two different accounts. This is a great service because it allows you to arrange to have a fraction of your pay put directly into savings. This means you will not see it or touch it before it is part of your savings. You always take it out, but it is much easier to save when the process is automatic like this.

If your employer does not offer to direct deposit to two accounts, you can always set-up a regular transfer from your checking to your saving account that works just the same. So you might schedule 10% of your paycheck to be transferred to saving on the 12th of every month. If your direct deposit to checking happens on the 10th of the month, then the transfer to savings will happen right after the money arrives from your employer.

This method is different because you pay Taxes first, Savings second, Expenses third, and Luxuries fourth. Now when you are getting to the end of the month you are going to cut back on luxuries instead of cutting back on savings.

The Smart Method

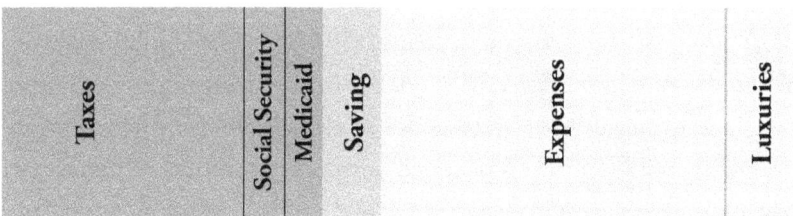

Taxes	Social Security	Medicaid	Saving	Expenses	Luxuries

This method will result in your savings growing much faster than the Hope Method above. You will be much less likely to shortchange your savings every month and much more likely to control spending on luxuries. This is a much more reliable path to wealth. But you can do even better.

The Brilliant Method

If your company offers a 401(K) or 403(B) pretax savings plan, then you need to take advantage of it. This account allows you to pay yourself, to save money, before you pay taxes. You have to open a special account to receive this money, but the process is very similar to opening a checking or savings account. We will provide more details on this account and more about its benefits in the next chapter. Right now we just want to show how it fits into a savings plan.

The 401(K) plan was created to allow people to save money tax-free as long as they agree to save it for a long time. Specifically, it is meant to help you save money for your retirement years. That is why it is called a Retirement Plan. But it is really a life-long wealth building plan. It just helps you get richer as you get older. The 403(B) plan is the same kind of account. It is just used by non-profit organizations like state and county governments who were not included in the original 401(K) law.

When you use the 401(K) plan to save money, the spending happens in this order Save first, Taxes second, Expenses third, Luxuries fourth. This looks almost the same as the Smart Method. But there is another benefit. Because you move money to your 401(K) before your taxes are computed—you are paying less taxes. The law was created to reduce the amount of money you pay to the government in taxes if you would agree to build your wealth over your working life. That is called an "incentive". Will you accept this gift of money?

The Brilliant Method—IRA

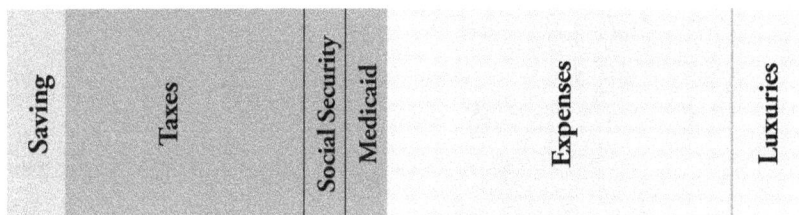

Saving	Taxes	Social Security	Medicaid	Expenses	Luxuries

↑

Tax Deferred

$30,000/year Salary
Put 6% in a IRA = $1,800/year = $150/month

You save $150
But your income only drops $112.50
WHY? No taxes paid on the $150

It is a bargain way to save.

Also if you earn 8%, that is $144 more.
In regular savings you would pay $36 in taxes
Here $0 right now.

FREE Money = $37.50*12 + $36 = $486

The effect is that you have more money in your hands if you use the 401(K) than if you put the same amount into a saving account on your own. There is really a new step between Saving and Taxes—I call it Free Money. That is the few extra dollars that will go to you instead of to the government because you are using the 401(K).

The Brilliant Method—401(K)

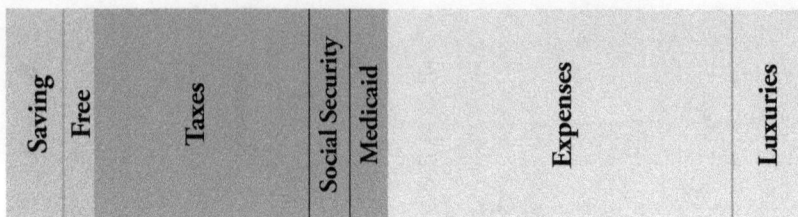

Saving — **Free** — **Taxes** — **Social Security** — **Medicaid** — **Expenses** — **Luxuries**

Employer Matching Funds
25% of the First 6%
Maybe 50%

$30,000/year Salary
Put 6% in a 401(K) = $1,800/year = $150/month

Free Matching = $37.50 or $75/month = $450 or $900/year
Matching = 2 years worth of raises

PLUS Tax Savings:
Taxes drop by $37.50/month

PLUS Earnings are Tax Deferred:
Earn 8% on $1800+$450 = $180 (save $45 in taxes)

Comparing the Three Methods

Now that you have a short understanding of all three methods of saving, let's look at an example of each so you can see the difference in the amount of money you have over a year. We are going to use an example of someone who is making $30,000 per year. That puts them in the 25% income tax bracket. I have assumed that their general bills are 60% of their take home pay.

Using the Hope Method of saving money last, this person will first pay bills and enjoy luxuries before attempting to save a few dollars. That would lead to a spending profile something like that shown in the table.

The Hope Method of Saving	
Gross Income	$2,500
Taxable Income	$2,500
Taxes–25%	$625
Social Security–7.65%	$191
Medicare–1.45%	$36
Bills	$1,500
Luxuries	$125
Total Spent	$2,478
Savings	**$23**
Savings Percentage	less than 1%

Just as you would suspect, people who live like this generally spend too much on luxuries and don't have enough left at the end of the month to save. Therefore, their savings and investing accounts are always empty of money, but their closet is full of clothes and their house is full of gadgets.

So let's look at this same person using the Smart Method of Saving. This time they direct deposit or automatically transfer 5% of their take home pay into a savings account every month. This happens before they start paying bills and it requires that they reign in their luxury spending.

The Smart Method of Saving	
Gross Income	$2,500
Taxable Income	$2,500
Taxes–25%	$625
Social Security–7.65%	$191
Medicare–1.45%	$36
Savings–5%	**$125**
Bills	$1,500
Total Spent	$2,478
Luxuries	$23
Savings Percentage	exactly 5%

Notice that this time the amount of money spent is exactly the same and most categories are the same. But the amounts in luxuries and savings have just switched places. Instead of spending $125 on luxuries every month, this person saves $125. But the pain come in when you notice that they only have $23 per month for luxuries. Sticking with a budget like this can be done, but it is going to be hard. It is something like a diet. Lots of people quit and everyone cheats.

This person could always find ways to reduce their bills and use that money for luxuries. The nice thing about putting a definite amount of saving first is that any money you can scrape together by cutting down on bills can be used for luxuries with much less guilt. The saving has already been done. But there is a better way than this.

If this person moves that same $125 from after-tax to pre-tax by putting it into a 401(K) plan, then something new happens. Since the $125 is not taxable, less money is taken away by Uncle Sam and a little extra money stays in the paycheck. In the table I have added a new item called "Free Money" to show how much this is.

The Brilliant Method of Saving	
Gross Income	$2,500
Savings via 401(K)–5%	**$125**
Taxable Income	$2,375
Taxes–25%	$594
Social Security–7.65%	$191
Medicare–1.45%	$36
Bills	$1,500
Total Spent	$2,321
Luxuries	$23
Free Money	**$31**
Savings Percentage	exactly 5%

With the Brilliant Method of Saving, you actually experience a rebate from Uncle Sam. You find $31 of free money in your account that was just not there in your after-tax saving plan. Where did it come from? If you look at the amount you paid in taxes, you will see that it is now $31 lower because you used a 401(K) plan. That money just did not leave your hands. You get to keep it—totally legally.

So under the Smart Plan the available spending money was $23. Under the Brilliant Plan it is $23 plus $31, or $54. So you are able to save $125 per month. But it just reduces your luxury money by $71. It still requires controlling your luxuries. But it is much more gentle than the Smart Method.

The lesson here is that you need to save money via a 401(K) plan if you can. It is more rewarding and less painful. But that is not the end. Once you succeed at working the Brilliant Plan for a few months or a year, you might want to try the All-in-One Plan.

The All-in-One Method

All-in-One simply means doing all three forms of saving simultaneously. It will drive you to a million dollars 50% faster than the Smart Method and 25% faster than the Brilliant Method. In this plan you save money in a 401(K). Then when you get paid you cut back on your bills a little and save that money. Then you decide to save the Free Money you got as a result of the 401(K) plan.

The All-in-One Method of Saving	
Gross Income	$2,500
Savings via 401(K)–5%	**$125**
Taxable Income	$2,375
Taxes–25%	$594
Social Security–7.65%	$191
Medicare–1.45%	$36

More Saving	$20
Bills	$1,480
Luxuries	$23
Free Money–Save It	$31
Total Spent	$2,375
Total Savings	$176
Savings Percentage	more than 7%

Doing all of this saving at the same time may sound extreme. It may sound too hard. It may sound obsessive. But there are extreme, obsessive, hard tackling people out there. They need a challenge to be happy. This plan is for all of you overachievers. It is also the next step in a progression. You might be stretching to do the Smart or Brilliant Method today. But in a few years, you might be doing so well that you are ready to handle the All-in-One Method.

Millionaire Employee Plan

If you are going to become wealthy as an employee you must do these things:

1) Put in top performance at work
2) Save 10% or more of your income
3) Pay off your credit card debt
4) Create a plan to pay off your house and car loans early
5) Learn to manage money and investments

There are many good ideas and little tricks to make this more effective. But these few things are the core of the Millionaire Employee plan.

Rule 5:

Invest

So what do you do with that money you captured in the savings plan? Well, it is only doing half of its job sitting in a sock drawer. The first half of its job is to ... NOT get spent. The second half of its job is to GROW, GROW, GROW. It cannot do its second half in a sock drawer. You need to learn a little bit about savings accounts and investment accounts. These are just as easy to create as your checking account—but they are going to do you a lot more good.

There is a lot to be learned about investing. But a few lessons are simple and easy to get your mind around. If you understand a checking account, then you understand a savings account. You are also just a stone's throw from understanding several other good investments.

Here is a list of the ABCs of Investment Options. These are the major avenues that you have to invest your money and grow it to one million dollars.

They are listed from simplest to most complex. They are also listed from lowest risk to highest risk.

1) Education
2) Savings Account
3) Certificates of Deposit
4) Money Market Funds
5) Bonds—Treasury and Corporate
6) Mutual Funds
7) Individual Stocks
8) Real Estate
9) Collectibles—Art, Antiques, etc.
10) Derivatives
11) Options
12) Commodities
13) Your Own Business—Franchise, Network, Self
14) Other Businesses—Direct Ownership

Everyone falls at a different place on this list. Some people cannot stand risk, others cannot stand security. Suze Orman says, *"you have to do what is right for you before you do what is right for your money."* That means you invest at the level of risk and the level of return where you are comfortable, where you can sleep at night and where your health is not effected. Do not make yourself miserable by insisting on investing like a high roller if you are not the kind of person who can handle the risk emotionally or financially. It is more important to be healthy and happy than it is to be wealthy.

It is important to find your comfort level and to find your area of interest. Everyone finds some kind of investing really interesting. If you are interested in one form of investment you will spend more time working on it, learning about it, and being successful at it.

Investment Options

You will notice that the first item on the list of investment options is "education". Money that you put into furthering your education is an investment. It will pay dividends for the rest of your life. As you heard in the Learn chapter of this book, we believe very strongly in the power and the necessity of an education in the 21st century. Each person needs to determine whether they have enough eduction to accomplish the goals they have for their life. If you need more education, by all means use the money you make to pay for more education. This is a decision that many people will make multiple times during their life. In the 19th century we all finished our education very young. In the 20th century, education was extended into our early 20's. In the 21st century, education is going to be part of successful people's lives for even longer.

The next set of options begins with creating a savings or a brokerage account where your money can accumulate. This is the home-base from which your investments will be launched. Many people make the mistake of treating their checking account as the foundation of their investments. Checking is where money is constantly going in and out. A savings or brokerage account is where money checks in, but it does not check out. It has a one-way door labeled "IN" and no door labeled "OUT".

Creating a savings account at a bank or a brokerage account with an investment firm is easy to do. If you opened a checking account, you can open a savings or brokerage account. I would recommend opening these accounts with well established brand companies. You will probably have a savings account at the same bank as your checking account. Your brokerage account should be at a company like Fidelity, Charles Schwab, Dreyfus, Edward Jones, or one of the other major players. When you are just starting out, do not open an account at a small boutique company that promises more personal service and more flexibility. You are not in a position to judge the stability or honesty of that company. You may be ready for them later in your life.

Once you are ready to invest your money there are literally thousands of options. If you are with one of the bigger companies like Fidelity you can talk to one of their advisors about your situation and they will describe the standard investment packages that are most appropriate for people like you. They are going to suggest putting your money in a combination of fixed income, bonds, and stocks.

The most important thing right now is that you are saving money and learning about investments. There are many more books which will talk you though selecting specific investments for your money. Your financial education is going to be a lifelong process. Your financial situation will be constantly changing. So you will be adjusting your investments as you grow older ... and as you grow richer.

The number one rule of investing is that you keep learning and keep investing for your entire life. The economy, the state of the world, your employment situation, and your emotional temperament will change what you are invested in. But you want your money making more money for you all the time.

IRA Plan

There is a difference between what assets your money is invested in and what legal account vehicles you are using. You can own bonds or stocks through many different vehicles—direct ownership, retirement plans, trusts, or corporations. Each of these offers different advantages and different limitations. Some of the money you are investing is meant to grow into a down payment for a house or a car. Some of the money is an emergency fund. Some of the money is for life-long wealth. Each of these calls for a different kind of vehicle.

When you save money your goal is to put that money to work making more money for you. It is like having an assistant who works for you, but who pays you for the privilege, rather than asking to be paid. You have a new employee, almost like a dependent. He or she will need some of your attention. She will depend on you to take care of her and grow her up to be a really big pocket of wealth. You are going to have to learn a little bit about "child raising", but that child is your money.

This book is about building life-long wealth. It is not about getting out of debt, though you should do that. It is not about the best way to buy a house, though you should learn about that. This book is about life-long wealth. It is about accumulating a million dollars and joining the ranks of the Millionaire Employee. One of best tools you have for accomplishing this is the Individual Retirement Account or IRA.

The IRA and the 401(K) are more powerful than just about anything else you can do when you are getting started investing. Why these so powerful? Because they both give you FREE money! Yes, that's right. If you use them you get more money for FREE. You don't have to work more. You don't have to get a raise. You just get money.

You are already saying, *"Wow, that is great. What's the catch?"* The catch is you **have** to save the money. You cannot spend it. You have to use it to build life-time wealth.

That does not sound so bad does it?

Remember when I told you to go to the front of the line in the savings chapter? I also told you that Uncle Sam is always in front of you in that line. He is the biggest bully in the country. He makes the rules and you have to follow them. When you get your paycheck you will see that there are lots of numbers on it. One of them is your Gross pay—the amount of money you technically earned for your work. Another number is your Net pay—that is the amount you actually take home with you. Standing between those two numbers are several automatic deductions that go straight to the Government. These guys **are** the front of the line. These guys get paid before you even see the check. They make your company take out their share and send it directly to them, and then give you what is left.

But there is a way to move yourself ALL THE WAY to the front of the line. There are programs that allow you to get paid before the Government is paid. This is a better place in the line than being second. But the really great part is that by moving in front of the Government, you do not have to pay taxes on the money you save.

People who are just getting started in their professional lives always significantly underestimate the effect that taxes have on their personal wealth. Taxes are generally the #1 largest expense that you will pay every single year. Taxes often cost more than your home mortgage payment. They are more than you car payments. More than all of the electronic toys you might buy … well for most of you. Anything you can do to reduce the taxes you pay puts that money directly into your pocket. You should choose to put that money into your savings and investment pocket.

Both an Individual Retirement Account (IRA) and a 401(K) plan (named after a specific section of the IRS legal code) allow you to pay your savings and investment account before the Government gets paid. And you get to pretend that you never earned that money. As far as the Government is concerned that money did not get paid to you this year and they are not going to tax it. So you save the money, and you get to keep a large percentage of it that you would have paid to the government as taxes.

How much FREE money can you get doing this? About 25% of whatever you put into the IRA or 401(K). So if you put $1,000 into these accounts, you will get about $250 for FREE. The only catch is that the $1,000 **has** to go into your investment account and stay there long enough to build real personal wealth. That sounds like a great catch, doesn't it. It is! So do it!

This program gets some people so excited that they want to put 50% of their paycheck into it every year. But their is an upper limit on this great deal. You can only avoid taxes on $5,000 a year in this account. But that can still save you $1,250 that would have gone out in taxes.

IRA Example

Let me give you an example. Imagine that you make a Gross salary of $3,000/month (that would be $36,000/year). When the IRS is at the front of the payment line, they are going to take 25% of this, or $750. Yikes! That is a lot of money! Yes, 25% is also known as one quarter of what you make. That is a **lot**. I am sorry to say that you are going to learn to get used to that. But I am happy to tell you that there are legal ways to lower that number. The easiest and best ways to get started are the IRA and 401(K).

First let's look at what happens when you are second in line to get paid, right behind the government. Let's assume you have decided to save $250 per month. We are going to omit all of the other automatic deductions that come from your check for now.

So you earned $3,000. The IRS took $750. And you saved $250. That leaves you with $2,000 to pay everyone else in the line—including those extra federal taxes we are not going to talk about right now.

The IRA lets you improve on this situation. Now let's look at the same situation when you are first in line, in front of the government.

You put that same $250 in savings into an IRA. You earn $3,000 for the month. Then you put $250 into your IRA. That leaves $2,750. Now the income taxes only apply to this smaller number. Your monthly taxes are $687.50 instead of $750. Look at that! The taxes dropped $62.50. So you now have $2,062.50 to pay everyone else in line. That $62.50 is FREE money. All you have to do is use the IRA to move your savings to the front of the line, before the government. And that is just in 1 month. You get to do that 12 times during a year, which adds up to $750 FREE dollars a year.

The beauty of the IRA? Everyone in the USA can do it. It is open to absolutely everyone who has an annual income. It does not take any special deals with your company. All you have to do is set-up an account at a bank or a brokerage company and get started. Also, this $250 per month is earning interest. It might be just 3%—or $7.50 per month. But that interest does not get taxed either. If you saved that $250 in a regular savings account and earned the same 3%, the government would want $1.88 of that $7.50 as income taxes.

If you use the IRA you will have **at least** an additional $842.70 in FREE money every year. For this example I used a monthly investment of just $250. The law allows you to do this with up to $5,000 per year, which is $417 per month. If you did that then the amount of FREE money you get in the first year goes up to $1,400! Now you tell me where else you can get someone to just **give** you $1,400 for FREE. Where? For most of us there is not a better deal.

401(K) Plan

The 401(K) plan is even better than the IRA. There is an additional limit in that the company you choose to work for has to create the plan for their employees. Luckily almost all professional employers have done this. It is such a great plan, that companies that do not do it have a hard time getting good employees to work for them. Once someone understands how powerful it is, the best people make sure they are working at a company that offers them a 401(K) plan.

With a 401(K) there are two major advantages even beyond what happens with an IRA. First, the upper limit per year on what you can put into it is $15,500. That is a lot higher than the $5,000 for an IRA. Second, many companies will **give** you matching funds if you will use the program. That's right they will just **give** you more money if you agree to save it instead of spend it. That is money that you were not going to get anyway, so how can you complain that they are **making** you save it, invest it, and build on that until you have become wealthy?

How much will they match you? Different companies do different amounts. But the most common number is 50% of the first 6% of your salary that you put into the 401(K) plan. What does that mean? For the person in the example who was earning $36,000 per year—the company is going to toss you an additional $1,080. Yep, that is the most common number. It can get even better than that. The only string attached is that you **have** to save it and use it to build life-time wealth. You cannot take it out and spend it next year.

As good as the 401(K) deal is, many people do not take advantage of it. In American companies that offer a 401(K) plan, only two-thirds of the employees are signed up for it. That means one third of the employees are choosing to take all of their money and spend it. Also, of the two-thirds that are using the program, only 10% of them are saving as much as they are allowed to. In some cases, the employees simply cannot survive on their income minus the 401(K) investment. But in many cases, people are choosing to live more luxuriously now and not trying to build lifetime wealth. That is not a good decision. That is **not** what you are going to choose.

Hanging Out

As a child you learned a lot just by being around your parents. You did not consciously realize that you were picking up habits, skills, personality traits, and beliefs that were being demonstrated by your parents. The same thing happens through your entire life. You learn to behave and think like the people you hang out with. This is a survival strategy. People learn behavior that appears to be successful. People learn behaviors that appear to be accepted by the people around them.

You have some control over your copy-cat behavior, but not complete control. You have seen people who will go to a party and insist on drinking soda while everyone else is downing beers. You will see them turn down multiple offers of beer and stick with soda over and over. But for 90% of these people they will eventually either switch to beer or switch to a different crowd. Very few stick with soda and stay with the beer crowd. It just doesn't work. Their personal compass is pointing one direction and the party crowd is pointing the other. Eventually they must go one way or the other. The whole time, their copy-cat gene is trying to mimic the behavior of whoever is around them.

Who do you hang out with? Are they wealthy? Are they trying to be? Do they know how? Are they helping you?

When you get to your job you will find people who are trying to get ahead just like you are. You will find people who do not care what happens. And you will find people who have already gotten ahead. Who can you learn from? The people who don't care? The people who don't know? Or the people who know how to do it and are doing it?

You learn from those people who have climbed the ladder ahead of you. There are many great ideas that have never been put into books. You can only get them from other people. There are many good and bad examples that you can only get from talking to people. Find out who is saving and investing their money successfully and choose to hang out with them. You want your copy-cat gene to learn from them.

Millionaire Benchmarks

Mark Victor Hansen, the *Chicken Soup for the Soul* guy, says there are four big Millionaire Benchmarks.

1) Achieving a Lifetime Income of $1M
2) Owning $1M worth of stuff (homes, cars, etc.)
3) Having a Positive Net Worth of $1M
4) Reaching a Yearly Income of $1M

Achieving a lifetime income of $1 million is basic math. How much do you earn per year? What is the average escalation of pay rate in your industry? Start adding up these numbers and you will know how many years have to pass for you to earn one million dollars in your lifetime. As I described earlier, if you are making $25,000 a year, it is just less than 40 years. At $50,000 it is 20 years. At $100,000 it is 10 years.

That is the first level.

The second level is owning $1 million worth of stuff. That means having a bank account, plus a house, plus cars, plus miscellaneous other things that are worth one million dollars. The second level ignores the debt you have accumulated to achieve control of all of these assets.

The third level is when all of your assets minus your debts add up to one million dollars. This means that if your house is worth $250,000, but you have a mortgage of $200,000, then that asset only contributes $50,000 to your net worth. At this level you have $1 million of assets above and beyond the total you have in debt. This is more challenging.

Finally, the fourth level is when you earn an annual income of $1 million. This is a very rare level of wealth. Mark Victor Hansen achieved it by writing the best selling *Chicken Soup* books. If you are an employee there are two primary ways that you could reach this level. First, you could have investments that perform extremely well and return a total of $1 million in a single year. If you started the year with $1 million in a start-up stock like Google, you might finish the year with that same stock, but it could them be worth $2 million. 99.9% of stocks never have a year like that. But that is one example. The second way an employee could reach level four is through their own small corporation. You might be running a business on the side that does very well and generates a million dollars in a year. But I suspect that if this does happen, you are not going to remain an employee much longer. You are going to need to spend all of your time on that newly successful small business.

Hansen's level one, two, and three are the kind of wealth we are setting you up for in this book. Level 4 is something special, something rare, and something beyond the Millionaire Employee plan. It is more the Millionaire Business Owner or the Millionaire Entrepreneur.

Mind of an Investor

If you are successful at earning a good salary and growing that salary every year. If you succeed in controlling your spending and enjoying what you get. If you are able to save 10% of your income, then you **are** going to accumulate a significant amount of money to invest. And your investments will be growing all your life. You will **have** to learn something about managing investments. You will **have** to know what investment opportunities are available, what the risks are with each, and which ones are best at different times.

Your life will be successful and wealthy enough that you really do need to learn to handle money. You need to have the mind of an investor.

Some people just hire everything out to a "professional". But there are a lot of professionals who are very poor at their jobs. There are others who are dishonest. You need to know enough to recognize who is good at it and to guide them along the path where you are comfortable.

Most standard investment advisors have a pie chart that shows where you should invest your money. This is the standard solution for everyone who is not involved in managing their own money. It is also the legally safe path for the advisor. He cannot be sued for losing money when he is following "standard industry practices".

At the beginning of your investing life this pie chart is probably fine for you. But over time as you accumulate more money you will have your own preferences for how your money is invested. Some of you will be very conservative and put everything into CDs, money markets, and treasury bonds. Others will be very aggressive and put everything into the stock market and hedge funds. Some of you will be real estate oriented and will buy rental properties.

Everyone has a different area of interest and comfort.

I cannot point you to specific stocks, bonds, real estate, and assets to put your money into. But I can tell you that part of your Millionaire Employee job is to learn to manage your own money.

There are some great books in these areas. I would start with the following. *The Intelligent Investor* by Benjamin Graham. This describes the philosophy of Value Investing. Ben Graham was the biggest advocate of this and his #1 disciple is Warren Buffet. If you have not heard that name before then you have been living in a hole for years. Warren Buffet is the richest man in the world. His current net worth is around $62 billion. Bill Gates is not the richest man in the world. In fact, he is currently #3 with $58 billion.

The Intelligent Investor describes the method and philosophy that Warren Buffet uses for his investments. Buffet is the CEO of an unusual company named Berkshire Hathaway. He uses this company to invest in other companies. Each year he writes an incredibly readable and insightful letter to his investors. It appears in the annual report of Berkshire Hathaway. It is not a book, but it is fantastic investing advice. You should get the annual report from the Berkshire Hathaway web site and read Buffet's letter every year.

The second book will be a much faster paced read. It is *Mad Money* by Jim Cramer. The advice that Cramer gives in this book is surprisingly similar to value investing. His advice is very level headed and sane—unlike his television show. He is not telling you which stocks to buy. He is showing you an approach to building your investment portfolio.

Finally, subscribe to *Money* magazine. It is a solid "Investing 101" manual. Each month they deal with investing issues for the young, the middle aged, and those near retirement.

The Automatic Millionaire by David Bach describes a financial plan for your life that is more detailed than this single chapter. He will give you a number of outstanding ideas for saving and investing your money.

I would also recommend *The Cash Flow Quadrant* by Robert Kiyosaki. In this book you learn to see the difference between a salaried employee, a professional service provider, an entrepreuner, and a business owner.

Finally, Suze Orman seems to be ruling the financial management roost right now. Her ideas and her books are very clear. I would recommend *Young, Fabulous, and Broke*—both the book and the PBS video.

Watch For One Year

If you are not ready to invest in the stock market, especially individual stocks, then I would recommend that you do some unique homework before you start. All investment advisers tell their clients that they have to know a company before they buy it. Jim Cramer says that if you own a stock you should spend 1 hour per week reading the info about that stock. You need to stay current on what they are doing.

However, most people do not know how to do that. How do you study a stock? What do you read? Jim Cramer lists a number of sources in his book *Mad Money* as a starter.

I would recommend that you pick a company that interests you. Something that you could motivate yourself to study for a year. Then spend a year reading anything you can find on that stock. Read their web site. Read the annual report. Read the quarterly reports. Setup a Google News Alert on the company name. Google it. Search for info online at the New York Times or other newspapers. Search for info about it in your local paper and in the newspaper that is local to the company's headquarters and to its largest facilities. Those local reporter are **very** interested in the company because it has a big impact on their local economy.

Finally, watch the stock price every day.

The goal of this year is not to decide to buy or short the stock. The goal is for you to understand where and how to find information about any company. The goal is for you to link the news you find with the stock price changes you see. The goal is for you to get a feel for what it is like to (1) research a company and (2) to know what makes the company a good buy or a bad buy. You start to see what makes the stock move. By the end of a year you should have some understanding of what kind of events are good for the company and what kind are bad. You will also begin to notice that the stock price moves before any official news comes out about the company. You will see the number of days ahead that the stock market anticipates the news.

At the end of the year you will be somewhat of an expert on that company. You should have some idea whether you would like to invest in it or know the good reasons that you should not. Some of this knowledge and your research behaviors can be transferred to any other stock. Many people choose to do their one year research project on the company they work for. It makes them aware of what is happening with that company in the larger outside world. It may also uncover some opportunities that they are in a position to take advantage of—such as a transfer to a new project or facility where their skills are needed.

Buy Stock Not Stuff

When you are ready to try your hand at individual stocks, you might put your money where your mouth is. Peter Lynch used to recommend that you invest in the companies you understand. Invest in companies that you already do business with.

Here is a variation on Lynch's advice.

You held onto your money by skipping one meal out, or a couple of sodas, or a pair of shoes. Maybe you can have your money and eat it too. We all eat thousands of dollars every year. Luckily we turn the money into food at a restaurant first. But it is the same thing as eating the money. We have the food and the restaurant has the money.

Do you like Italian food? Seafood? Steaks? Do you ever eat at the Olive Garden, Red Lobster, or Longhorn Steakhouse? These all belong to Darden Restaurants Incorporated (DRI). Darden has been a very successful business. With the money you have saved by turning down one meal out at a Darden restaurant, why don't invest in Darden? Instead of buying the food you buy the company. If everyone is like you and likes to eat at these restaurants, then they should have plenty of business from all of the people who do not read this book. If Darden stock is selling at $50 per share and you skip two meals there, that is a share of their stock. So you take the money in your savings or investment account and buy a couple of shares every month. Now because of the brokerage transaction fees, it is better to buy in larger blocks every few months or once a year. If you do this, where has the money gone? You ate it! Or at least mentally consider that you ate it and it is gone.

If you do that then it does not matter if the stock goes up or down. You were going to eat that money at the restaurant anyway. Now you own part of the company that makes the food you like. You keep doing this and you will soon have a nice little nest egg made up of the companies that you do business with daily. I did this myself. I bought Darden stock in place of dinner. I bought Apple stock in place of a new iPod. I bought Game Stop instead of a new video game. And I bought Exxon stock instead of the gas to drive down to the shopping center where I was going to buy the other stuff.

Now I own a few shares of all of these companies. And I got them using money that would have been spent on their products. If the stocks do go to zero I have not lost anything on Darden and Exxon. Their products would have been used up long ago. I would have lost a little on Apple and Game Stop since their products would have still been in my house. But, I am certain that over the long haul all of these stocks are not going to zero. They are selling their goods to millions of other people just like me and I think they will continue to do a good job at that.

Note on stock purchases: It is a little expensive to place an order for 1 share of Darden at $50. You will pay $50 for the stock and around $10 to the brokerage company to make the trade for you. That is a 20% fee for the trade—that is more expensive than credit card interest. This idea works best if you put the money in a Money Market account and do one larger purchase at the end of the year—like 12 shares for $600. The brokerage fee will still be $10, but it will only represent 1.5% of the purchase price instead of 20%.

If you follow the advice we have given up to this point you WILL find yourself with a substantial pool of savings. You will be wondering how to invest that. You will need to become knowledgeable about investing. You will have one of the best problems that anyone can have.

Understanding investments well enough to do them yourself or to intelligently farm them out to a professional is part of your future. It is not something that only the rich and the old do—it is something that the Millionaire Employee does as well.

Rule 6:

Incorporate

T he last step in our plan is for you to incorporate yourself. There are so many financial and tax benefits to becoming your own corporation that it is impossible to list all of them. In fact, it is almost impossible to imagine all of them.

Even while you are working for your major employer—that's the one that pays you dependably, provides the great 401(K) program, and gives you access to their insurance rates—you can still own, control, and run your own corporation.

The purpose of incorporating is to make more money than you do during your day job. This is often called "Multiple Streams of Income". It is a very powerful approach to business and wealth. It is also very empowering personally. Having your own small company teaches you what it really takes to run a business and make money. It pulls your head out of the small cog job you have during the day and puts you head in the CEO seat at night. You start to understand the challenges and the opportunities that are all around you.

It is thrilling. It is refreshing. It is challenging. And it is rewarding, both financially and personally.

At the very least this corporation will do the same thing for you that the 401(K) and IRA did—it will give you FREE money that you were going to pay to the government in taxes anyway. That is the effect **before** you even start making money in your little venture.

I have operated my own small corporation while holding a full-time job for over 10 years. During that time I have worked for 5 different companies. My corporation has earned thousands of dollars which allowed me to live better than my coworkers. It also allowed me to invest in bigger ventures which my regular coworkers could not. And finally I was able to deduct business expenses which my coworkers could not.

At an age when my neighbors were taking vacations to visit their parents in Georgia, I was taking my family to London, Paris, and Rome. My children are in high school and they have already visited twelve different countries in Europe, Asia, and the Caribbean. I could have done this with debt—which is how a lot of people do it. But, I did it with the money I earned from my own company. Your corporation can make a significant positive impact on your lifestyle if you find something that can make money.

This company saved me thousands of dollars in taxes by making my business expenses directly deductible from my income. Many of these deductions were simply impossible as an individual employee, but were completely legal as a corporation.

America is extremely friendly to the idea of starting your own company. There are a number of different forms of incorporation to make this easier. There are government programs that will give you advice and will help you with loans. In America we believe in opportunity and we know that these opportunities often start with the creation of a small business.

There are a number of different kinds of corporations in the U.S. Each is created with a different type of entity in mind and each offers slightly different advantages. You can choose from the ABCs of Incorporating:

1) **DBA or "Doing Business As".** This just requires you to pick a name for the business, print some business cards, and open a checking account. No more paperwork than that in many states. You have essentially just given yourself a nick-name and you are using that to identify your business. You see lots of these on the sides of service trucks—"Ron's Lawn Service", "Trees by Tony", "Skipper Clippers", and the list goes on and on.

2) **Network Marketing.** Companies like Amway® and Nutrilife® allow you to hook up with an existing business and become a small part of something that is already working. Richard Kiyosaki calls this buying into an existing business system. You learn to do business their way.

3) **Sole Proprietorships** allow you to become the sole owner of a business. This is sometimes just another name for a DBA.

4) **Limited Liability Corporations or LLC's** allow you to create a company with its own Tax ID Number, called an Employer ID Number, but still run the revenue from the company through your own tax return.

5) **S-Corp** is a miniaturized version of the major C-Corporation. It creates an independent entity which has one or more owners. Money earned by the S-Corp can be held in the company or passed to the investors, owners, and employees.

6) **Professional Services Corporations** are for doctors, medical providers, and people who provide a service that is licensed by the state or other entity.

7) **Limited Liability Partnerships** are for accountants and lawyers. You probably do not need one of these.

8) **C-Corporation** is what most big companies are. This is IBM, Apple, and GM. This one is probably not for you … not yet.

9) **Real Estate Investment Trust** is for buying and selling real estate through a group of investors or partners.

My business started while teaching at a university. When you have a Ph.D. in your pocket you naturally gravitate toward learning and the university. Most people who have a doctorate degree find themselves working as an Adjunct Professor or Instructor at a local university—just for the fun of teaching. They go back to college where they spent so much of their time and where they are very comfortable. They get into the classroom as the instructor. They have many years experience watching instructors, so they naturally step to the front of the class to do what they have seen dozens of other professors do.

This was my first step into "Multiple Streams of Income". I started teaching night courses at local universities. I taught students how to build computer simulations and games. We talked about software design, modeling, and programming. As an Adjunct Professor I was earning between $1,800 and $2,800 each semester for teaching one course. I taught for 3 hours one night a week and spent another 3 to 5 hours preparing for the lecture and grading assignments. The money is not too bad, but nothing to get rich on. But the big advantage of this second stream of income was that I could use it as I wanted. It was not really part of my budget. I typically used it to fund a vacation. So I was able to enjoy a very nice week with my family and all it cost me was about 6 hours per week during a 15 week semester. We Ph.D. types also get a kick out of teaching, so I was having fun at the same time.

Then I realized that this class material would make a great professional seminar for people who were already in their careers. So I joined up with a company that offered seminars in that specific area and had my own small company to manage the money that I earned from them. I found this to be a fantastic benefit. I was already spending hundreds of dollars every year on journals and books to keep up with my profession. But now I needed that same information to be able to create the content for my seminars. It was suddenly a deductible business expense. It cost the same amount to buy those materials. But I could now deduct that money from my earned income and reduce my taxes by 28 cents for every dollar I spent on the materials.

So in addition to making a little more money, I was now deducting expenses that I was already incurring.

Ahh Haaa! So that is what people mean when they talk about tax advantages to businesses that normal people can't take advantage of. But I needed some form of corporation to help me do this right. Two accountants and my own research showed that the LLC was the best way to handle this business. As a result, I have been teaching seminars and writing books through this LLC for more than ten years, and have enjoyed the tax benefits that go with this.

I did not start big. As I said my first year as an Adjunct Professor I taught two semesters at $1,800 each, so I made an additional $3,600. When I went into the seminar business, my first year I only made $12,000. But it was a good start. I learned how to be a business, how to handle the paperwork, and how to look for opportunities. But every year the amount of money that I made went up.

The LLC turns a second income and its supporting expenses into part of your salary. It can reduce the amount of taxes you pay by expensing the things you have to buy anyway.

LLC Tax Deductions

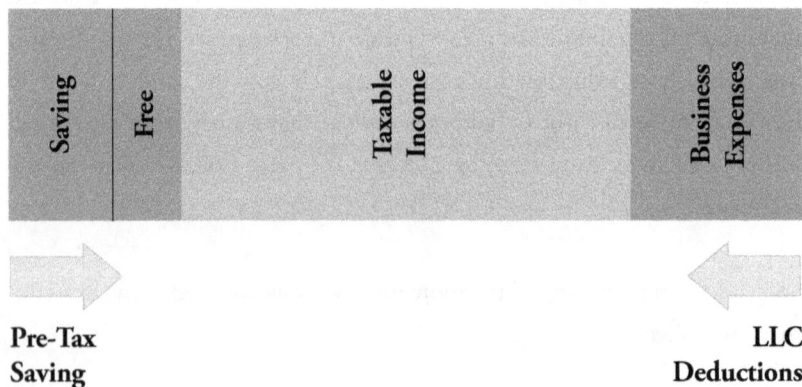

Saving	Free		Taxable Income		Business Expenses

Pre-Tax Saving   **LLC Deductions**

Be The Boss

If you do not have an idea for a business, I would not recommend starting an LLC. What would you call it? What would you describe it as on your paperwork? How would it help you on your taxes?

Incorporating is the step you take after you get started. After you have shown you can make some money with your idea. It is not the first thing you do.

You might be eager to create the corporation just so you can have the tax advantages immediately. I would not recommend that. The IRS isn't stupid. They have seen every trick in the book. If they think you are just creating this company to write-off your hobbies, they are going to come and get you.

So, don't rush after a tax advantage until you are actually making money at something.

Eventually you are going to want to run your own company. I would highly recommend doing it on the side first to find out how much work it is—to find out how well you like it—to find out if there is any real money there—BEFORE you quit your day job.

Once you get started, you are going to:

1) Understand business as an owner,
2) Learn about the paperwork and regulations,
3) Understand taxes at a new level,
4) Find legal tax deductions,
5) Find out if you are any good at being the boss of yourself or other people, and
6) Have a great time learning, growing, and earning.

More Tax Free Saving

It took me a couple of years before I realized that I could save more money in my corporation by using a tax deferred savings plan, just like the 401(K) that I had at my day job. Congress and the IRS had created these same advantages for small business owners and it was possible to take advantage of those as well as my personal 401(K) plan at work.

The ins-and-outs of doing this can get complicated. So I turned to a professional for help. I used an accountant to get everything started. Then I turned to TurboTax Home & Business to keep it going. The accountant charged way too much and TurboTax was only about $100 per year. One of the features it offers is determining which of these deferred savings plans is most advantageous and legal for my corporation to use on top of my personal plans. These include:

1) Self Employed 401(K)
2) SEP
3) SIMPLE
4) Roth IRA

You can learn more about each of these inside of the TurboTax software, on the IRS web site, on the Wikipedia web site, or reading books.

Books

I read a number of books on running my own company and on creating an LLC. These helped a little. But none of them were a good substitute for just getting started and figuring it out as you go along. When you need to learn something to get your job done, you learn pretty fast. You also sidestep all of the mumbo jumbo and get right to the HOW TO part of getting the job done and moving on.

Honestly, there is more good information on the IRS web site than in most of the books.

Network Marketing

Some business advisers recommend that one path into owning and running a business is to join a networking marketing company like Amway®, Nutralife®, Prepaid Legal Services®, etc. Robert Kiyosaki of *Rich Dad, Poor Dad* fame says that this is a way to buy into a business model that someone else has created. It is a way to learn to do business with mentors and an existing system.

Many people have made their fortunes with these systems. But I have never met one of them. I have met people who are trying, but never anyone who has succeeded.

I tried it myself, and found that it just did not fit my personality, my lifestyle, or my goals. I cannot recommend this. It does not work for me and is not part of the professional workplace, a.k.a. your day job—which is where these organizations expect you to hunt for customers and future associates. You cannot market your network business at your day job and expect to keep your day job. It is a conflict of interest for which companies will reprimand you and perhaps fire you.

Charlatans

The Greek philosopher Dio Chrysostom observed quite accurately,

"Why oh why are human beings so hard to teach, but so easy to deceive?"

America is about opportunity. We sometimes get ourselves into trouble by allowing people to pursue opportunity, like the financial crisis we are in right now. But our fundamental philosophy is that individuals have the right to pursue their own happiness and to create their own businesses ventures. We believe that the government exists to help people in doing this, not to prevent it, and not to approve it.

The government has created a number of paths for you to build your own business and improve your personal future. This information is available very cheaply in government publications, web sites, trade books, and seminars.

There is nothing secret or underhanded about this in America. Unfortunately, there are charlatans who preach that they have secret documents and programs that they will set up for you. They offer something special that the normal citizen does not know about. If you will just give them a few thousand dollars they will get you set up to make millions using their secrets. These guys are charlatans. They are rip-off artists.

You do not have to sneak down dark alleys in America to start a business and benefit from the advantages of having one. That is not how America works.

Do not go for these plans. They are created just to make the slick tongued salesman rich. You need to be the opposite of Chrysostom's worries. You need to be, *"Hard to Deceive and Easy to Teach."* If you are easy to teach and quick to learn, you will be equipping yourself to be hard to deceive.

Get Started

There are millions of millionaire employees in this country. They did not get that way playing basketball, acting on television, or winning the lottery. They took control of their education, their career, and their money. They started building, often at a young age like you, and in a relatively short time they became millionaires. Relatively short does not mean one or two years. You just don't get your hands on enough money in one or two years to get to a million. Also, you do not have the power of compounding investments over time to get you there in two years. Relatively short means ten years or fifteen years or twenty years.

When you are 22 or 25 that sounds like a very long time. But really, it is just the time it took you to get from Middle School to college graduation. Can you conjure up a memory from Middle School? How long ago does that feel like? It often feels just a little longer than what you did last summer.

Your life is a great adventure and you are going to want to do bigger things every year. But without working on your personal wealth you are going to have a hard time affording it. You can spend all of your money on new clothes and new electronic gadgets now. Or you can spend half and save half, so that when you are ready to spend a week in London or a month on safari you can afford it.

If you build this wealth you are also going to find a very strange and surprising idea in your head. You are going to begin to wonder if you can be a John D. Rockefeller that creates enough wealth to make you and the next generation of your family into millionaires. Are you going to be able to make your kids rich before they are adults? You might start to think that you can actually be a small Andrew Carnegie, Bill Gates, or Warren Buffet.

That is a very strange thought. That is a huge mental step from where you are right now. But it is also realistic. It can happen to you. You can achieve success of that stature by starting your professional life with a college degree in your pocket, a job with benefits that allow you to save and invest, and a plan to build your wealth over a lifetime.

You all have the seeds of the future in your minds, hands, and hearts. You are going to be the most successful generation in history. This financial crisis is a great time to get started. It has been very rough on those of us with investments and assets. But it is a huge opportunity for you to start when things are cheap.

Go out there and get started living like a Millionaire Employee.

Quick Start Worksheet

This worksheet will get you started thinking like a Millionaire Employee. You will capture a snapshot of your career and financial world. Seeing this on paper in a simple form will be a big help in starting the process. Most people carry all of this around in the fuzzy, dark, shifting box that is their brain. Nothing is clear in there and every thought is continually interrupted by dozens of others. You have to bring this out of the fuzzy dark and onto the bright light of paper.

You are the only person who is going to see this paper. It is not an assignment. You are not turning it in. You will not share it with other people. BE HONEST. Do not try to hide facts from yourself. The urge to hide facts from yourself should set off the alarm that something is wrong.

Earning

This group of factors determines how much money you earn and how that will grow over time.

Your education is a first and essential step in determining how much you earn.

Education
Degrees. What degrees have you earned or are you earning? Also list areas of specializations and minors.
Certifications. Have you earned any special certifications from associations or groups that control employment in your field?
Seminars. What seminars have you attended that gave you knowledge and insight into a field or practice that you can apply after college?
Self Study Topics. Are you studying professional, financial, or self improvement topics on your own? Include any where you have read 3 or more books.

Becoming the Millionaire Employee

Education Habit. Describe what your habit has been in pursuing an education. Who controls what you learn? Are you active in pursuing knowledge or guided by others?

Employment

Career/Professional Area. What area do you consider to be your profession, career, or focus? What are the starting salaries in these areas?

Hours Per Week. How many hours are you working per week? How many do you expect to work in your career area?

Professionals You Know. Who do you know in these fields? Do you know them well enough to make an appointment to talk with them about the field?

Associations. List some associations or societies that people in your field belong to. Have you joined these?

Character Traits. What do you consider to be your dominant character traits?

Love It. Does this field really excite you? Can you imagine working in it for 5 to 10 years? List some other fields that you really find attractive and exciting.

If you already have a paycheck, then get it out and enter the numbers in one of the columns. If you do not have a paycheck, then project an annual salary and use the percentages below.

Income			
	Weekly (52/year)	Bi-Weekly (26/year)	Monthly (12/year)
Pay Check (Gross)			
Federal Taxes (25%)			
State & Local Taxes (0%)			
OAHI Medicare (1.45%)			
OASI Social Security (7.65%)			
Insurance			
401(K) Retirement			
Take Home Pay (Net)			

*To convert from Weekly to Bi-Weekly, multiply by 2. To convert from Bi-Weekly to Monthly multiply by 2.17. Some people get paid every 4 weeks. In this case, change the monthly number to 13/year. The multiplier from Bi-Weekly is then 2.

Spending

This group of factors identifies where your money goes. Some expenses arise monthly, others weekly, and others yearly. Just enter the numbers into the appropriate column, and then convert to Monthly. We are going to do all comparisons on a Monthly basis.

Bills			
	Weekly (52/year)	Monthly (12/year)	Yearly (1/year)
Rent or Mortgage			
Property Taxes			
Car Payment #1			
Car Payment #2			
Home Insurance			
Auto Insurance			
Other Insurance			
Electricity			
Water			
Television (Cable, Satellite)			
Movies (Netflix, Theater)			
Gaming (WoW)			
Memberships (Gym)			
Subscriptions (Magazines)			
Cell Phone			
Wired Phone			
Groceries			
Eating Out			
Gas and Tolls			

Total Bills			

To convert from Weekly to Monthly multiply by 4.3. To convert from Yearly to Monthly divide by 12. If your Monthly pay is actually every 4 weeks in the Income section above, then change 12/year to 13/year. Then the Weekly to Monthly multiple is 4. Yearly to Monthly is divide by 13.

From each paycheck, how much to you regularly or automatically put into some form of savings?

Saving			
	Weekly (52/year)	Bi-Weekly (26/year)	Monthly (12/year)
Auto Deposit to Savings			
Manual Transfer to Savings			
401(K) Contribution			
IRA Contribution			
Stock Brokerage Account			
Treasury Bonds			
Total Savings			

*To convert from Weekly to Bi-Weekly, multiply by 2. To convert from Bi-Weekly to Monthly multiply by 2.17. Some people get paid every 4 weeks. In this case, change the monthly number to 13/year. The multiplier from Bi-Weekly is then 2.

Growing

The items in this section look a lot like the savings section. However, they extend those ideas from just capturing the money and holding onto it, to really making that money grow over the long-term.

From each paycheck, how much do you regularly or automatically put into some form of savings?

Investing			
	Weekly (52/year)	Monthly (12/year)	% of Net Income
Savings Account			
Certificate of Deposit			
401(K) / IRA			
Stock Brokerage Account			
Treasury Bonds			
Real Estate			
Business			
Total Investing			

*To convert from Weekly to Bi-Weekly, multiply by 2. To convert from Bi-Weekly to Monthly multiply by 2.17. Some people get paid every 4 weeks. In this case, change the monthly number to 13/year. The multiplier from Bi-Weekly is then 2.

What do you really know about your tax situation?

Taxes
Federal Income Tax. What is your federal income tax rate? You can calculate this from the income numbers above or look it up in the tax tables at the end.
State and Local Income Tax. Are state and local income taxes deducted from your check? What percent? You can calculate this from the Income section above.
Deductions. Do you know how much you can contribute tax-free to a 401(K) or IRA? Do you have college tuition that you can deduct? Did you know you can deduct interest on a home loan?
Incorporate. Did you know you can create your own corporation and turn normal and necessary professional expenses into tax deductions? Do you know what an LLC and S-Corp are?

2008 IRS Tax Tables

Schedule X—If your filing status is **Single**

If your taxable income is:		The tax is:	of the amount over—
Over—	But not over—		
$0	$7,550	----------- 10%	$0
7,550	30,650	$755.00 + 15%	7,550
30,650	74,200	4,220.00 + 25%	30,650
74,200	154,800	15,107.50 + 28%	74,200
154,800	336,550	37,675.50 + 33%	154,800
336,550	-----------	97,653.00 + 35%	336,550

Schedule Y-1—If your filing status is **Married filing jointly** or **Qualifying widow(er)**

If your taxable income is:		The tax is:	of the amount over—
Over—	But not over—		
$0	$15,100	----------- 10%	$0
15,100	61,300	$1,510.00 + 15%	15,100
61,300	123,700	8,440.00 + 25%	61,300
123,700	188,450	24,040.00 + 28%	123,700
188,450	336,550	42,170.00 + 33%	188,450
336,550	-----------	91,043.00 + 35%	336,550

Schedule Y-2—If your filing status is **Married filing separately**

If your taxable income is:		The tax is:	
Over—	*But not over—*		*of the amount over—*
$0	$7,550	---------- 10%	$0
7,550	30,650	$755.00 + 15%	7,550
30,650	61,850	4,220.00 + 25%	30,650
61,850	94,225	12,020.00 + 28%	61,850
94,225	168,275	21,085.00 + 33%	94,225
168,275	----------	45,521.50 + 35%	168,275

Schedule Y-2—If your filing status is **Head of household**

If your taxable income is:		The tax is:	
Over—	*But not over—*		*of the amount over—*
$0	$10,750	---------- 10%	$0
10,750	41,050	$1,075.00 + 15%	10,750
41,050	106,000	5,620.00 + 25%	41,050
106,000	171,650	21,857.50 + 28%	106,000
171,650	336,550	40,239.50 + 33%	171,650
336,550	----------	94,656.50 + 35%	336,550